THE
GOD
BOOK

By Mike Murdock

Wisdom is the principal thing; therefore get wisdom:
and with all thy getting get understanding.
Proverbs 4:7

Wisdom International
P.O. Box 747
Dallas, Texas 75221

Unless otherwise indicated, all Scripture quotations are taken from the *King James Version* of the Bible.

The God Book
ISBN 1-56394-004-3
Copyright © 1990 by Mike Murdock
P.O. Box 99
Dallas, Texas 75221

Published by
Wisdom International
P.O. Box 747
Dallas, Texas 75221

DEDICATION

To my mother and father, John Ellis Murdock, Sr. and Willie Murdock who diligently taught me the ways of God, and to my only son, Michael Jason Murdock whom I pray will be mightily used of God to heal the wounds of his generation.

TABLE OF CONTENTS

Section 5

HIS PERCEPTION

Section 6

HIS PERSONALITY

Section 7

HIS PERSONHOOD

ELOHIM	God Almighty
JEHOVAH	God Who Lives
EL SHADDAI	All Encompassing God
ADONAI	My God, My Father
JEHOVAH JIREH	My Provider
JEHOVAH M'KADDESH	My Sanctifier
JEHOVAH NISSI	God My Banner
JEHOVAH ROPHE.........................	My Healer
JEHOVAH SHALOM	My Peace
JEHOVAH TSIDKENU	God My Righteousness
JEHOVAH ROHI	God My Shepherd
JEHOVAH SHAMMAH	God Is There
EL ELYON	The Most High God
JEHOVAH TSEBAOTH....................	The Lord of Hosts
JEHOVAH MAKKEH	The Lord Our Smiter
JEHOVAH GMOLAH	The God of Recompenses
JEHOVAH ELONHAY......................	The Lord My God
EL-ELOHE-ISRAEL	The Personal God Of Israel
JEHOVAH ELOHEENU	The Lord, Our God

Section 8

HIS PLACE

Section 9

HIS PLANS

Section 10

HIS POWER

Section 11

HIS POWER OVER DEMONS

Section 16

HIS PRESENCE

Section 17

HIS PROFILE

Section 18

HIS PROMISES

Section 19
HIS PROSPERITY

Section 20
HIS PROTECTION OF HIS CHILDREN

Section 21
HIS PURITY

Section 22
HIS PURPOSE FOR MAN ON EARTH

Section 23
HIS PURSUIT OF MAN

His Pain

WHAT IS GOD'S OPINION OF ABORTION?

Thou shalt not kill.   *Exodus 20:13*

Lo, children are an heritage of the Lord: and the fruit of the womb is his reward.

As arrows are in the hand of a mighty man; so are children of the youth.

Happy is the man that hath his quiver full of them: they shall not be ashamed, but they shall speak with the enemies in the gate.   *Psalms 127:3-5*

For thou hast possessed my reins: thou hast covered me in my mother's womb.

I will praise thee; for I am fearfully and wonderfully made: marvellous are thy works; and that my soul knoweth right well.

My substance was not hid from thee, when I was made in secret, and curiously wrought in the lowest parts of the earth.

Thine eyes did see my substance, yet being unperfect; and in thy book all my members were written, which in continuance were fashioned, when as yet there was none of them.

How precious also are thy thoughts unto me, O God! how great is the sum of them!

If I should count them, they are more in number than the sand: when I awake, I am still with thee.   *Psalm 139:13-18*

Thou art worthy, O Lord, to receive glory and honour and power: for thou hast created all things, and for thy pleasure they are and were created.   *Revelation 4:11*

QUESTION 2 — WHAT IS GOD'S OPINION OF ALCOHOLISM?

Wine is a mocker, strong drink is raging: and whosoever is deceived thereby is not wise. *Proverbs 20:1*

Be not among winebibbers; among riotous eaters of flesh:

For the drunkard and the glutton shall come to poverty: and drowsiness shall clothe a man with rags.

Who hath woe? who hath sorrow? who hath contentions? who hath babbling? who hath wounds without cause? who hath redness of eyes?

They that tarry long at the wine; they that go to seek mixed wine.

Look not thou upon the wine when it is red, when it giveth his colour in the cup, when it moveth itself aright.

At the last it biteth like a serpent, and stingeth like an adder.

Thine eyes shall behold strange women, and thine heart shall utter perverse things.

Yea, thou shalt be as he that lieth down in the midst of the sea, or as he that lieth upon the top of a mast.

They have stricken me, shalt thou say, and I was not sick; they have beaten me, and I felt it not: when shall I awake? I will seek it yet again. *Proverbs 23:20,21,29-35*

And be not drunk with wine, wherein is excess; but be filled with the Spirit; *Ephesians 5:18*

QUESTION 3
WHAT IS GOD'S OPINION OF CHILD ABUSE?

Lo, children are an heritage of the Lord: and the fruit of the womb is his reward.

As arrows are in the hand of a mighty man; so are children of the youth.

Happy is the man that hath his quiver full of them: they shall not be ashamed, but they shall speak with the enemies in the gate. *Psalm 127:3-5*

At the same time came the disciples unto Jesus, saying, Who is the greatest in the kingdom of heaven?

And Jesus called a little child unto him, and set him in the midst of them,

And said, Verily I say unto you, Except ye be converted, and become as little children, ye shall not enter into the kingdom of heaven.

Whosoever therefore shall humble himself as this little child, the same is greatest in the kingdom of heaven.

But whoso shall offend one of these little ones which believe in me, it were better for him that a millstone were hanged about his neck, and that he were drowned in the depth of the sea

Even so it is not the will of your Father which is in heaven, that one of these little ones should perish.

Matthew 18:1-4, 6, 14

QUESTION 4
WHAT IS GOD'S OPINION OF DIVORCE?

And the Pharisees came to him, and asked him, Is it lawful for a man to put away his wife? tempting him.

And he answered and said unto them, What did Moses command you?

And they said, Moses suffered to write a bill of divorcement, and to put her away.

And Jesus answered and said unto them, For the hardness of your heart he wrote you this precept.

But from the beginning of the creation God made them male and female.

What therefore God hath joined together, let not man put asunder.   *Mark 10:2-6, 9*

Defraud ye not one the other, except it be with consent for a time, that ye may give yourselves to fasting and prayer; and come together again, that Satan tempt you not for your incontinency.

And unto the married I command, yet not I, but the Lord, Let not the wife depart from her husband:

But to the rest speak I, not the Lord: If any brother hath a wife that believeth not, and she be pleased to dwell with him, let him not put her away.

And the woman which hath an husband that believeth not, and if he be pleased to dwell with her, let her not leave him.

For the unbelieving husband is sanctified by the wife, and the unbelieving wife is sanctified by the husband: else were your children unclean; but now are they holy.

But if the unbelieving depart, let him depart. A brother or sister is not under bondage in such cases: but God hath called us to peace.

For what knowest thou, O wife, whether thou shalt save thy husband? or how knowest thou, O man, whether thou shalt save thy wife?

Art thou bound unto a wife? seek not to be loosed. Art thou loosed from a wife? seek not a wife.

I Corinthians 7:5, 10, 12-16, 27

Submitting yourselves one to another in the fear of God.

Wives, submit yourselves unto your own husbands, as unto the Lord.

Husbands, love your wives, even as Christ also loved the church, and gave himself for it;

So ought men to love their wives as their own bodies. He that loveth his wife loveth himself.

Nevertheless let every one of you in particular so love his wife even as himself; and the wife see that she reverence her husband. *Ephesians 5:21, 22, 25, 28, 33*

Wives, submit yourselves unto your own husbands, as it is fit in the Lord.

Husbands, love your wives, and be not bitter against them.
Colossians 3:18, 19

QUESTION 5 | WHAT IS GOD'S OPINION OF HOMOSEXUALITY?

Thou shalt not lie with mankind, as with womankind: it is abomination. *Leviticus 18:22*

If a man also lie with mankind, as he lieth with a woman, both of them have committed an abomination: they shall surely be put to death; their blood shall be upon them. *Leviticus 20:13*

QUESTION 6 | WHAT IS GOD'S REACTION TO LYING?

The lip of truth shall be established for ever: but a lying tongue is but for a moment. *Proverbs 12:19*

5

Wherefore putting away lying, speak every man truth with his neighbour: for we are members one of another.

Ephesians 4:25

QUESTION 7 — WHAT IS GOD'S OPINION OF STEALING?

Thou shalt not steal. *Exodus 20:15*

Ye shall not steal, neither deal falsely, neither lie one to another. *Leviticus 19:11*

Let him that stole steal no more: but rather let him labour, working with his hands the thing which is good, that he may have to give to him that needeth. *Ephesians 4:28*

But let none of you suffer as a murderer, or as a thief, or as an evildoer, or as a busybody in other men's matters.

I Peter 4:15

His Past

QUESTION 8 — WHO IS GOD?

And God said unto Moses, I AM THAT I AM: and he said, Thus shalt thou say unto the children of Israel, I AM hath sent me unto you. *Exodus 3:14*

And God spake all these words, saying,
I am the LORD thy God, which have brought thee out of the land of Egypt, out of the house of bondage.
Thou shalt have no other gods before me. *Exodus 20:1-3*

Ye are my witnesses, saith the LORD, any my servant whom I have chosen: that you may know and believe me, and understand that I am he: before me there was no God formed, neither shall there be after me. *Isaiah 43:10*

Thus saith the LORD the King of Israel, and his redeemer the LORD of hosts; I am the first, and I am the last; and beside me there is no God. *Isaiah 44:6*

In the beginning was the Word, and the Word was with God, and the Word was God.
The same was in the beginning with God. *John 1:1,2*

But to us there is but one God, the Father, of whom are all things, and we in him; and one Lord Jesus Christ, by whom are all things, and we by him. *I Corinthians 8:6*

Who is the image of the invisible God, the firstborn of every creature:

For by him were all things created, that are in heaven, and that are in earth, visible and invisible, whether they be thrones, or dominions, or principalities, or powers: all things were created by him, and for him:

And he is before all things, and by him all things consist.

And he is the head of the body, the church: who is the beginning, the firstborn from the dead; that in all things he might have the preeminence. *Colossians 1:15-18*

And he said unto me, It is done. I am Alpha and Omega, the beginning and the end. I will give unto him that is athirst of the fountain of the water of life freely. *Revelation 21:6*

QUESTION 9 WHERE DID GOD COME FROM?

In the beginning God created the heaven and the earth.
Genesis 1:1

In the beginning was the Word, and the Word was with God, and the Word was God.

The same was in the beginning with God.

All things were made by him; and without him was not any thing made that was made.

In him was life; and the life was the light of men.

He was in the world, and the world was made by him, and the world knew him not. *John 1:1-4, 10*

Without father, without mother, without descent, having neither beginning of days, nor end of life; but made like unto the Son of God; abideth a priest continually. *Hebrews 7:3*

Who is the image of the invisible God, the firstborn of every creature:

For by him were all things created, that are in heaven, and that are in earth, visible and invisible, whether they be thrones, or dominions, or principalities, or powers: all things were created by him and for him:

And he is before all things, and by him all things consist.

And he is the head of the body, the church: who is the beginning, the firstborn from the dead; that in all things he might have the preeminence. *Colossians 1:15-18*

And when I saw him, I fell at his feet as dead. And he laid his right hand upon me, saying unto me, Fear not; I am the first and the last: *Revelation 1:17*

QUESTION
10 HOW OLD IS GOD?

But the LORD shall endure for ever: *Psalm 9:7a*

Before the mountains were brought forth, or ever thou hadst formed the earth and the world, even from everlasting to everlasting, thou art God. *Psalm 90:2*

But thou, O LORD, shalt endure for ever; and thy remembrance unto all generations.

I said, O my God, take me not away in the midst of my days: thy years are throughout all generations.

But thou art the same, and thy years shall have no end.
Psalm 102: 12, 24, 27

In the beginning was the Word, and the Word was with God, and the Word was God.

The same was in the beginning with God. *John 1:1,2*

Jesus said unto them, Verily, verily, I say unto you, Before Abraham was, I am. *John 8:58*

Who is the image of the invisible God, the firstborn of every creature:
And he is before all things, and by him all things consist. *Colossians 1:15, 17*

Being born again, not of corruptible seed, but of incorruptible, by the word of God, which liveth and abideth for ever. *I Peter 1:23*

I am the Alpha and Omega, the beginning and the ending, saith the Lord, which is, and which was, and which is to come, the Almighty. *Revelation 1:8*

3
His Penalties

QUESTION
11 WILL GOD JUDGE US FOR
UNFORSAKEN SINS?

And I will punish the world for their evil, and the wicked
for their iniquity; and I will cause the arrogancy of the proud to
cease, and will lay low the haughtiness of the terrible.

Isaish 13:11

But the children of the kingdom shall be cast out into outer
darkness: there shall be weeping and gnashing of teeth.

Matthew 8:12

In the day when God shall judge the secrets of men by Jesus
Christ according to my gospel. *Romans 2:16*

Be not deceived; God is not mocked: for whatsoever a man
soweth, that shall he also reap. *Galatians 6:7*

And I saw the dead, small and great, stand before God; and
the books were opened: and another book was opened, which
is the book of life: and the dead were judged out of those things
which were written in the books, according to their works.

And the sea gave up the dead which were in it; and death
and hell delivered up the dead which were in them: and they
were judged every man according to their works.

Revelation 20:12, 13

But the fearful, and unbelieving, and the abominable, and
murderers, and whoremongers, and sorcerers, and idolaters, and
all liars, shall have their part in the lake which burneth with fire
and brimstone: which is the second death. *Revelation 21:8*

12 WHAT ANGERS GOD?

Ye shall not go after other gods, of the gods of the people which are round about you;

(For the LORD thy God is a jealous God among you) lest the anger of the LORD thy God be kindled against thee, and destroy thee from off the face of the earth.

Deuteronomy 6:14, 15

And the LORD was angry with Solomon, because his heart was turned from the LORD God of Israel, which had appeared unto him twice, *I Kings 11:9*

And there they burnt incense in all the high places, as did the heathen whom the LORD carried away before them; and wrought wicked things to provoke the LORD to anger:

For they served idols, whereof the LORD had said unto them, Ye shall not do this thing. *II Kings 17: 11, 12*

God judgeth the righteous, and God is angry with the wicked every day. *Psalm 7:11*

13 WHAT DOES GOD SAY ABOUT THE PERSON WHO DOES NOT BELIEVE HE EXISTS?

So are the paths of all that forget God; and the hypocrite's hope shall perish: *Job 8:13*

The wicked shall be turned into hell, and all the nations that forget God. *Psalm 9:17*

The fool hath said in his heart, There is no God. They are corrupt, they have done abominable works, there is none that doeth good.   *Psalm 14:1*

He that believeth on him is not condemned: but he that believeth not is condemned already, because he hath not believed in the name of the only begotten Son of God.   *John 3:18*

QUESTION 14 HOW DOES GOD FEEL ABOUT PREMARITAL OR EXTRAMARITAL SEX?

Ye have heard that it was said by them of old time, Thou shalt not commit adultery:

But I say unto you, That whosoever looketh on a woman to lust after her hath committed adultery with her already in his heart.   *Matthew 5:27-28*

Watch and pray, that ye enter not into temptation: the spirit indeed is willing, but the flesh is weak.   *Matthew 26:41*

But now I have written unto you not to keep company, if any man that is called a brother be a fornicator, or covetous, or an idolater, or a railer, or a drunkard, or an extortioner; with such an one no not to eat.   *I Corinthians 5:11*

But if they cannot contain, let them marry: for it is better to marry than to burn.

But if any man think that he behaveth himself uncomely toward his virgin, if she pass the flower of her age, and need so require, let him do what he will, he sinneth not: let them marry.

Nevertheless he that standeth steadfast in his heart, having no necessity, but hath power over his own will, and hath so decreed in his heart that he will keep his virgin, doeth well.
                                                              I Corinthians 7:9, 36, 37

There hath no temptation taken you but such as is common to man: but God is faithful, who will not suffer you to be tempted above that ye are able; but will with the temptation also make a way to escape, that ye may be able to bear it.

I Corinthians 10:13

QUESTION 15 DOES GOD PUNISH PEOPLE FOR THEIR SINS?

Know therefore that the LORD thy God, he is God, the faithful God, which keepeth covenant and mercy with them that love him and keep his commandments to a thousand generations;

And repayeth them that hate him to their face, to destroy them: he will not be slack to him that hateth him, he will repay them to his face. *Deuteronomy 7:9-10*

The Lord preserveth all them that love him: but all the wicked will he destroy. *Psalm 145:20*

And I will punish the world for their evil, and the wicked for their iniquity; and I will cause the arrogancy of the proud to cease, and will lay low the haughtiness of the terrible.

Isaiah 13:11

Then shall he say also unto them on the left hand, Depart from me, ye cursed, into everlasting fire, prepared for the devil and his angels: *Matthew 25:41*

4
His People

16 WHY DID GOD MAKE MAN?

And God said, Let us make man in our image, after our likeness: and let them have dominion over the fish of the sea, and over the fowl of the air, and over the cattle, and over all the earth, and over every creeping thing that creepeth upon the earth.

And God blessed them, and God said unto them, Be fruitful, and multiply, and replenish the earth, and subdue it: and have dominion over the fish of the sea, and over the fowl of the air, and over every living thing that moveth upon the earth.

Genesis 1:26, 28

What is man, that thou art mindful of him? and the son of man, that thou visitest him?

For thou hast made him a little lower than the angels, and hast crowned him with glory and honour.

Thou madest him to have dominion over the works of thy hands; thou hast put all things under his feet:

All sheep and oxen, yea, and the beasts of the field;

The fowl of the air, and the fish of the sea, and whatsoever passeth through the paths of the seas.   *Psalm 8:4-8*

For ye are the temple of the living God; as God hath said, I will dwell in them, and walk in them; and I will be their God, and they shall be my people.

And will be a Father unto you, and ye shall be my sons and daughters, saith the Lord Almighty.   *II Corinthians 6:16b, 18*

Having predestinated us unto the adoption of children by Jesus Christ to himself, according to the good pleasure of his will,

To the praise of the glory of his grace, wherein he hath made us accepted in the beloved.

That we should be to the praise of his glory, who first trusted in Christ. *Ephesians 1:5, 6, 12*

And hath raised us up together, and made us sit together in heavenly places in Christ Jesus:

That in the ages to come he might shew the exceeding riches of his grace in his kindness toward us through Christ Jesus.

For by grace are ye saved through faith; and that not of yourselves: it is the gift of God:

Not of works, lest any man should boast.

For we are his workmanship, created in Christ Jesus unto good works, which God hath before ordained that we should walk in them. *Ephesians 2:6-10*

But ye are a chosen generation, a royal priesthood, an holy nation, a peculiar people; that ye should shew forth the praises of him who hath called you out of darkness into his marvellous light: *I Peter 2:9*

Thou art worthy, O Lord, to receive glory and honour and power: for thou hast created all things, and for thy pleasure they are and were created. *Revelation 4:11*

17 WHY DID GOD MAKE WOMAN?

but for Adam there was not found an help meet for him.

And the LORD God caused a deep sleep to fall upon Adam, and he slept: and he took one of his ribs, and closed up the flesh instead thereof;

And the rib, which the LORD God had taken from man, made he a woman, and brought her unto the man.

And Adam said, This is now bone of my bones, and flesh of my flesh: she shall be called Woman, because she was taken out of Man.

Therefore shall a man leave his father and his mother, and shall cleave unto his wife: and they shall be one flesh.

Genesis 2:20b-24

Who can find a virtuous woman? for her price is far above rubies.

The heart of her husband doth safely trust in her, so that he shall have no need of spoil.

She will do him good and not evil all the days of her life.

Proverbs 31:10-12

Now concerning the things whereof ye wrote unto me: It is good for a man not to touch a woman.

Nevertheless, to avoid fornication, let every man have his own wife, and let every woman have her own husband.

Let the husband render unto the wife due benevolence: and likewise also the wife unto the husband.

The wife hath not the power of her own body, but the husband: and likewise also the husband hath not the power of his own body, but the wife. *I Corinthians 7:1-4*

18 WHAT WERE THE FIRST WORDS THAT GOD EVER SPOKE TO MAN?

And God blessed them, and God said unto them, Be fruitful, and multiply, and replenish the earth, and subdue it: and have dominion over the fish of the sea, and over the fowl of the air, and over every living thing that moveth upon the earth.

Genesis 1:28

19 HOW DOES GOD FEEL ABOUT ME?

Are not two sparrows sold for a farthing? and one of them shall not fall on the ground without your Father.

But the very hairs of your head are all numbered.

Fear ye not therefore, ye are of more value than many sparrows. *Matthew 10:29-31*

20 HOW LONG DOES GOD EXPECT US TO PRAY EACH DAY?

And he cometh unto the disciples, and findeth them asleep, and saith unto Peter, What, could ye not watch with me one hour? *Matthew 26:40*

And he spake a parable unto them to this end, that men ought always to pray, and not to faint; *Luke 18:1*

Watch ye therefore, and pray always, that ye may be accounted worthy to escape all these things that shall come to pass, and to stand before the Son of man. *Luke 21:36*

Praying always with all prayer and supplication in the Spirit, and watching thereunto with all perseverance and supplication for all saints; *Ephesians 6:18*

Pray without ceasing. *I Thessalonians 5:17*

QUESTION
21 DOES GOD REALLY HEAR EVERY PRAYER?

If my people, which are called by my name, shall humble themselves, and pray, and seek my face, and turn from their wicked ways; then will I hear from heaven, and will forgive their sin, and will heal their land. *II Chronicles 7:14*

Thou shalt make thy prayer unto him, and he shall hear thee, and thou shalt pay thy vows. *Job 22:27*

But verily God hath heard me; he hath attended to the voice of my prayer. *Psalm 66:19*

Call unto me, and I will answer thee, and shew thee great and mighty things, which thou knowest not. *Jeremiah 33:3*

But thou, when thou prayest, enter into thy closet, and when thou hast shut the door, pray to thy Father which is in secret; and thy Father which seeth in secret shall reward thee openly.

But when ye pray, use not vain repetitions, as the heathen do: for they think that they shall be heard for their much speaking.

Be not ye therefore like unto them: for your Father knoweth what things ye have need of, before ye ask him.

19

After this manner therefore pray ye: Our Father which art in heaven, Hallowed be thy name.   *Matthew 6:6-9*

Therefore I say unto you, What things soever ye desire, when ye pray, believe that ye receive them, and ye shall have them.   *Mark 11:24*

For the eyes of the Lord are over the righteous, and his ears are open unto their prayers: but the face of the Lord is against them that do evil.   *I Peter 3:12*

And this is the confidence that we have in him, that, if we ask any thing according to his will, he heareth us:
And if we know that he hear us, whatsoever we ask, we know that we have the petitions that we desired of him.
                                                       I John 5:14-15

QUESTION 22 | WHAT IS GOD'S OPINION OF OUR WEAKNESSES?

For he knoweth our frame; he remembereth that we are dust.   *Psalm 103:14*

Strengthen ye the weak hands, and confirm the feeble knees.
Say to them that are of a fearful heart, Be strong, fear not: behold, your God will come with vengeance, even God with a recompense; he will come and save you.   *Isaiah 35:3,4*

He giveth power to the faint; and to them that have no might he increaseth strength.
Even the youths shall faint and be weary, and the young men shall utterly fall:

But they that wait upon the LORD shall renew their strength; they shall mount up with wings as eagles; they shall run, and not be weary; and they shall walk, and not faint.
Isaiah 40:29-31

Let the weak say, I am strong. *Joel 3:10b*

For when we were yet without strength, in due time Christ died for the ungodly. *Romans 5:6*

And he said unto me, My grace is sufficient for thee: for my strength is made perfect in weakness. Most gladly therefore will I rather glory in my infirmities, that the power of Christ may rest upon me. *II Corinthians 12:9*

For consider him that endured such contradiction of sinners against himself, lest ye be wearied and faint in your minds.
Hebrews 12:3

QUESTION 23 DOES GOD CONSIDER ONE RACE SUPERIOR TO ANOTHER?

Then Peter opened his mouth, and said, Of a truth I perceive that God is no respecter of persons:
But in every nation that feareth him, and worketh righteousness, is accepted with him. *Acts 10:34-35*

And hath made of one blood all nations of men for to dwell on all the face of the earth, and hath determined the times before appointed, and the bounds of their habitation;
Forasmuch then as we are the offspring of God, we ought not to think that the Godhead is like unto gold, or silver, or stone, graven by art and man's device. *Acts 17:26, 29*

Is he the God of the Jews only? is he not also of the Gentiles?
Yes, of the Gentiles also: *Romans 3:29*

For there is no difference between the Jew and the Greek:
for the same Lord over all is rich unto all that call upon him.
                                              Romans 10:12

There is neither Jew nor Greek, there is neither bond nor
free, there is neither male nor female: for ye are all one in
Christ Jesus.   *Galatians 3:28*

And have put on the new man, which is renewed in
knowledge after the image of him that created him:
Where there is neither Greek nor Jew, circumcision nor
uncircumcision, Barbarian, Scythian, bond nor free: but Christ
is all, and in all.   *Colossians 3:10, 11*

And they sung a new song, saying, Thou art worthy to take
the book, and to open the seals thereof: for thou wast slain, and
hast redeemed us to God by thy blood out of every kindred,
and tongue, and people, and nation;   *Revelation 5:9*

After this I beheld, and, lo, a great multitude, which no
man could number, of all nations, and kindreds, and people,
and tongues, stood before the throne, and before the Lamb,
clothed with white robes, and palms in their hands;
                                              Revelation 7:9

QUESTION 24 — DOES GOD TALK TO PEOPLE?

And they heard the voice of the LORD God walking in the
garden in the cool of the day: and Adam and his wife hid
themselves from the presence of the LORD God amongst the
trees of the garden.   *Genesis 3:8*

And when the LORD saw that he turned aside to see, God called unto him out of the midst of the bush, and said, Moses, Moses. And he said, Here am I.   *Exodus 3:4*

And the LORD said unto Moses, Thus thou shalt say unto the children of Israel, Ye have seen that I have talked with you from heaven.   *Exodus 20:22*

And the LORD spake unto you out of the midst of the fire: ye heard the voice of the words, but saw no similitude; only ye heard a voice.   *Deuteronomy 4:12*

Out of heaven he made thee to hear his voice, that he might instruct thee: and upon earth he shewed thee his great fire; and thou heardest his words out of the midst of the fire.
                    Deuteronomy 4:36

And thine ears shall hear a word behind thee, saying, This is the way, walk ye in it, when ye turn to the right hand, and when ye turn to the left.   *Isaiah 30:21*

And there came a voice from heaven, saying, Thou art my beloved Son, in whom I am well pleased.   *Mark 1:11*

It is the spirit that quickeneth; the flesh profiteth nothing: the words that I speak unto you, they are spirit, and they are life.   *John 6:63*

My sheep hear my voice, and I know them, and they follow me: *John 10:27*

When Moses saw it, he wondered at the sight: and as he drew near to behold it, the voice of the Lord came unto him,
                    Acts 7:31

For as many as are led by the Spirit of God, they are the sons of God. *Romans 8:14*

He that hath an ear, let him hear what the Spirit saith unto the churches. *Revelation 3:13*

QUESTION 25 — IN WHAT WAY HAS GOD COMMUNICATED WITH PEOPLE?

And ere the lamp of God went out in the temple of the LORD, where the ark of God was, and Samuel was laid down to sleep;

And the LORD came, and stood, and called as at other times, Samuel. Then Samuel answered, Speak; for thy servant heareth. *I Samuel 3:3, 10*

And there was a cloud that overshadowed them: and a voice came out of the cloud, saying, This is my beloved Son: hear him. *Mark 9:7*

Howbeit when he, the Spirit of truth, is come, he will guide you into all truth: for he shall not speak of himself; but whatsoever he shall hear, that shall he speak: and he will shew you things to come. *John 16:13*

God, who at sundry times and in divers manners spake in time past unto the fathers by the prophets,

Hath in these last days spoken unto us by his Son, whom he hath appointed heir of all things, by whom also he made the worlds; *Hebrews 1:1,2*

See that ye refuse not him that speaketh. For if they escaped not who refused him that spake on earth, much more shall not we escape, if we turn away from him that speaketh from heaven:
Hebrews 12:25

And I saw another angel fly in the midst of heaven, having the everlasting gospel to preach unto them that dwell on the earth, and to every nation, and kindred, and tongue, and people,
Revelation 14:6

QUESTION 26 — HOW DOES A PERSON BECOME GOOD ENOUGH TO LIVE WITH GOD?

Whosoever therefore shall confess me before men, him will I confess also before my Father which is in heaven.

But whosoever shall deny me before men, him will I also deny before my Father which is in heaven. *Matthew 10:32, 33*

But as many as received him, to them gave he power to become the sons of God, even to them that believe on his name:
John 1:12

Him that cometh to me I will in no wise cast out.
John 6:37b

Let not your heart be troubled: ye believe in God, believe also in me.

In my Father's house are many mansions: if it were not so, I would have told you. I go to prepare a place for you.

And if I go and prepare a place for you, I will come again, and receive you unto myself; that where I am, there ye may be also. *John 14:1-3*

But these are written, that ye might believe that Jesus is the Christ, the Son of God; and that believing ye might have life through his name. *John 20:31*

That if thou shalt confess with thy mouth the Lord Jesus, and shalt believe in thine heart that God hath raised him from the dead, thou shalt be saved.

For with the heart man believeth unto righteousness; and with the mouth confession is made unto salvation.

Romans 10:9,10

He that cometh to God must believe that he is, and that he is a rewarder of them that diligently seek him. *Hebrews 11:6b*

If we confess our sins, he is faithful and just to forgive us our sins, and to cleanse us from all unrighteousness. *I John 1:9*

5
His Perception

WHAT IS GOD'S PERCEPTION OF THE FAMILY?

Only take heed to thyself, and keep thy soul diligently, lest thou forget the things which thine eyes have seen, and lest they depart from thy heart all the days of thy life: but teach them thy sons, and thy sons' sons; *Deuteronomy 4:9*

And these words, which I command thee this day, shall be in thine heart:
And thou shalt teach them diligently unto thy children, and shalt talk of them when thou sittest in thine house, and when thou walkest by the way, and when thou liest down, and when thou risest up. *Deuteronomy 6:6,7*

Therefore shall ye lay up these my words in your heart and in your soul, and bind them for a sign upon your hand, that they may be as frontlets between your eyes.
And ye shall teach them your children, speaking of them when thou sittest in thine house, and when thou walkest by the way, when thou liest down, and when thou risest up.
Deuteronomy 11:18,19

Lo, children are an heritage of the LORD: and the fruit of the womb is his reward.
As arrows are in the hand of a mighty man; so are children of the youth.
Happy is the man that hath his quiver full of them: they shall not be ashamed, but they shall speak with the enemies in the gate. *Psalms 127:3-5*

Train up a child in the way he should go: and when he is old, he will not depart from it. *Proverbs 22:6*

The father of the righteous shall greatly rejoice: and he that beggetteth a wise child shall have joy of him. *Proverbs 23:24*

And all thy children shall be taught of the LORD; and great shall be the peace of thy children. *Isaiah 54:13*

Wives, submit yourselves unto your own husbands, as unto the Lord.
For the husband is the head of the wife, even as Christ is the head of the church: and he is the saviour of the body. *Ephesians 5:22-23*

But if any provide not for his own, and specially for those of his own house, he hath denied the faith, and is worse than an infidel. *I Timothy 5:8*

QUESTION
28 WHAT IS GOD'S PERCEPTION OF TIME?

Before the mountains were brought forth, or ever thou hadst formed the earth and the world, even from everlasting to everlasting, thou art God.
For a thousand years in thy sight are but as yesterday when it is past, and as a watch in the night. *Psalms 90:2,4*

He appointed the moon for seasons: the sun knoweth his going down. *Psalms 104:19*

To everything there is a season, and a time to every purpose under the heaven: *Ecclesiastes 3:1*

But, beloved, be not ignorant of this one thing, that one day is with the Lord as a thousand years, and a thousand years as one day.   *II Peter 3:8*

QUESTION 29 | WHAT IS GOD'S PERCEPTION OF MARRIAGE?

And the LORD God said, It is not good that the man should be alone; I will make him an help meet for him.

Therefore shall a man leave his father and his mother, and shall cleave unto his wife: and they shall be one flesh.
Genesis 2:18,24

Whoso findeth a wife findeth a good thing, and obtaineth favour of the LORD.   *Proverbs 18:22*

But from the beginning of the creation God made them male and female.

What therefore God hath joined together, let not man put asunder.   *Mark 10:6,9*

Submitting yourselves one to another in the fear of God.

Wives, submit yourselves unto your own husbands, as unto the Lord.

Husbands, love your wives, even as Christ also loved the church, and gave himself for it;

So ought men to love their wives as their own bodies. He that loveth his wife loveth himself.

Nevertheless let every one of you in particular so love his wife even as himself; and the wife see that she reverence her husband.   *Ephesians 5:21,22,25,28,33*

Wives, submit yourselves unto your own husbands, as it is fit in the Lord.

Husbands, love your wives, and be not bitter against them.

Colossians 3:18,19

QUESTION 30
WHAT IS GOD'S PERCEPTION OF CHILDREN?

Lo, children are an heritage of the LORD: and the fruit of the womb is his reward.

As arrows are in the hand of a mighty man; so are children of the youth.

Happy is the man that hath his quiver full of them: they shall not be ashamed, but they shall speak with the enemies in the gate. *Psalms 127:3-5*

Children's children are the crown of old men; and the glory of children are their fathers. *Proverbs 17:6*

But whoso shall offend one of these little ones which believe in me, it were better for him that a millstone were hanged about his neck, and that he were drowned in the depth of the sea.

Take heed that ye despise not one of these little ones; for I say unto you, That in heaven their angels do always behold the face of my Father which is in heaven. *Matthew 18:6,10*

But Jesus said, Suffer little children, and forbid them not, to come unto me: for of such is the kingdom of heaven.

Matthew 19:14

Verily I say unto you, Whosoever shall not receive the kingdom of God as a little child, he shall not enter therein.

And he took them up in his arms, put his hands upon them, and blessed them. *Mark 10:15-16*

QUESTION 31

WHAT IS GOD'S PERCEPTION OF GOVERNMENT AND AUTHORITY?

Daniel answered and said, Blessed be the name of God for ever and ever: for wisdom and might are his:

And he changeth the times and the seasons: he removeth kings, and setteth up kings: he giveth wisdom unto the wise, and knowledge to them that know understanding.

He revealeth the deep and secret things: he knoweth what is in the darkness, and the light dwelleth with him.

Daniel 2:20-22

Let every soul be subject unto the higher powers. For there is no power but of God: the powers that be are ordained of God.

Whosoever therefore resisteth the power, resisteth the ordinance of God: and they that resist shall receive to themselves damnation.

For rulers are not a terror to good works, but to the evil. Wilt thou then not be afraid of the power? do that which is good, and thou shalt have praise of the same:

For he is the minister of God to thee for good. But if thou do that which is evil, be afraid; for he beareth not the sword in vain: for he is the minister of God, a revenger to execute wrath upon him that doeth evil.

Wherefore ye must needs be subject, not only for wrath, but also for conscience sake.

For this cause pay ye tribute also: for they are God's ministers, attending continually upon this very thing.

Render therefore to all their dues: tribute to whom tribute is due; custom to whom custom; fear to whom fear; honour to whom honour.

Romans 13:1-7

6
His Personality

WHAT IS GOD'S CHARACTER AND PERSONALITY?

Who is like unto thee, O LORD, among the gods? who is like thee, glorious in holiness, fearful in praises, doing wonders?
Exodus 15:11

And the LORD passed by before him, and proclaimed, The LORD, The LORD God, merciful and gracious, longsuffering, and abundant in goodness and truth,
For thou shalt worship no other god: for the LORD, whose name is Jealous, is a jealous God: *Exodus 34:6, 14*

God is not a man, that he should lie; neither the son of man, that he should repent: hath he said, and shall he not do it? or hath he spoken, and shall he not make it good?
Numbers 23:19

The LORD is gracious, and full of compassion; slow to anger, and of great mercy.
The LORD is good to all: and his tender mercies are over all his works. *Psalms 145:8-9*

To whom then will ye liken me, or shall I be equal? saith the Holy One. *Isaiah 40:25*

For I am the LORD, I change not; therefore ye sons of Jacob are not consumed. *Malachi 3:6*

O righteous Father, the world hath not known thee: but I have known thee, and thee have known that thou hast sent me.
John 17:25

Then Peter opened his mouth, and said, Of a truth I perceive that God is no respecter of persons:
Acts 10:34

QUESTION 33 DOES GOD LAUGH OR HAVE A SENSE OF HUMOR?

He that sitteth in the heavens shall laugh: the Lord shall have them in derision.
Psalms 2:4

And if so be that he find it, verily I say unto you, he rejoiceth more of that sheep, than of ninety and nine which went not astray.
Matthew 18:13

QUESTION 34 WHAT BRINGS PLEASURE TO GOD?

Fear not, little flock; for it is you Father's good pleasure to give you the kingdom.
Luke 12:32

For it is God which worketh in you both to will and to do of his good pleasure.
Philippians 2:13

Thou art worthy, O Lord, to receive glory and honour and power: for thou hast created all things, and for thy pleasure they are and were created.
Revelation 4:11

QUESTION 35

WILL GOD HELP ME FIGHT MY BATTLES?

For the LORD your God is he that goeth with you, to fight for you against your enemies, to save you.   *Deuteronomy 20:4*

And all this assembly shall know that the LORD saveth not with sword and spear: for the battle is the LORD's, and he will give you into our hands.   *I Samuel 17:47*

The LORD shall go forth as a mighty man, he shall stir up jealousy like a man of war: he shall cry, yea, roar, he shall prevail against his enemies.

I have long time holden my peace; I have been still, and refrained myself: now will I cry like a travailing woman; I will destroy and devour at once.   *Isaiah 42:13,14*

Who is this King of glory? The LORD strong and mighty, the LORD mighty in battle.   *Psalms 24:8*

QUESTION 36

WHAT WERE THE FIRST WORDS RECORDED GOD EVER SPOKE?

In the beginning God created the heaven and the earth.

And the earth was without form, and void; and darkness was upon the face of the deep. And the Spirit of God moved upon the face of the waters.

And God said, Let there be light: and there was light.

And God saw the light, that it was good: and God divided the light from the darkness.

And God called the light Day, and the darkness he called Night. And the evening and the morning were the first day.

Genesis 1:1-5

QUESTION 37 DOES GOD HAVE FAVORITE COLORS?

Moreover thou shalt make the tabernacle with ten curtains of fine twined linen, and blue, and purple, and scarlet: with cherubims of cunning work shalt thou make them.

And thou shalt make an hanging for the door of the tent, of blue, and purple, and scarlet, and fine twined linen, wrought with needlework.

Exodus 26:1,36

And thou shalt make the breastplate of judgment with cunning work; after the work of the ephod thou shalt make it; of gold, of blue, and of purple, and of scarlet, and of fine twined linen, shalt thou make it.

Exodus 28:15

Them hath he filled with wisdom of heart, to work all manner of work, of the engraver, and of the cunning workman, and of the embroiderer, in blue, and in purple, in scarlet, and in fine linen, and of the weaver, even of them that do any work, and of those that devise cunning work.

Exodus 35:35

They put upon the fringe of the borders a ribband of blue:

Numbers 15:38b

And he made the veil of blue, and purple, and crimson, and fine linen, and wrought cherubims thereon.

II Chronicles 3:14

Where were white, green, and blue, hangings, fastened with cords of fine linen and purple to silver rings and pillars of marble:

the beds were of gold and silver, upon a pavement of red, and blue, and white, and black, marble. *Esther 1:6*

He made the pillars thereof of silver, the bottom thereof of gold, the covering of it of purple, the midst thereof being paved with love, for the daughters of Jerusalem. *Song of Solomon 3:10*

And the building of the wall of it was of jasper: and the city was pure gold, like unto clear glass.

And the foundations of the wall of the city were garnished with all manner of precious stones. The first foundation was jasper; the second, sapphire; the third, a chalcedony; the fourth, an emerald;

The fifth, sardonyx; the sixth, sardius; the seventh, chrysolyte; the eighth, beryl; the ninth, a topaz; the tenth, a chrysoprasus; the eleventh, a jacinth; the twelfth, an amethyst.

And the twelve gates were twelve pearls: every several gate was of one pearl: and the street of the city was pure gold, as it were transparent glass. *Revelation 21:18-21*

7
His Personhood

QUESTION
38

WHAT ARE THE DIFFERENT NAMES OF GOD MENTIONED IN THE BIBLE?

ELOHIM .... GOD ALMIGHTY
JEHOVAH .... GOD WHO LIVES
EL SHADDAI .... ALL ENCOMPASSING GOD
ADONAI .... MY GOD, MY FATHER
JEHOVAH JIREH .... MY PROVIDER
JEHOVAH M'KADDESH .... MY SANCTIFIER
JEHOVAH NISSI .... GOD MY BANNER
JEHOVAH ROPHE .... MY HEALER
JEHOVAH SHALOM .... MY PEACE
JEHOVAH TSIDKENU ..... GOD MY RIGHTEOUSNESS
JEHOVAH ROHI .... GOD MY SHEPHERD
JEHOVAH SHAMMAH .... GOD IS THERE
EL ELYON .... THE MOST HIGH GOD
JEHOVAH TSEBAOTH .... THE LORD OF HOSTS
JEHOVAH MAKKEH .... THE LORD OUR SMITER
JEHOVAH GMOLAH ... THE GOD OF RECOMPENSES
JEHOVAH ELONHAY.................... THE LORD MY GOD
EL-ELOHE-ISRAEL . THE PERSONAL GOD OF ISRAEL
JEHOVAH ELOHEENU .... THE LORD, OUR GOD

ELOHIM - GOD ALMIGHTY - The God of total might and power, covenant maker, creative and sovereign One.

And they shall be my people, I will be their God:
Jeremiah 32:38

For by him were all things created, that are in heaven, and that are in earth, visible and invisible, whether they be thrones, or dominions, or principalities, or powers: all things were created by him, and for him: *Colossians 1:16*

JEHOVAH - GOD WHO LIVES - The revealing One Who is unchangeable, the I AM.

And when the LORD saw that he turned aside to see, God called unto him out of the midst of the bush, and said, Moses, Moses. And he said, Here am I.

And he said, Draw not nigh hither: put off thy shoes from off thy feet, for the place whereon thou standest is holy ground.

Moreover he said, I am the God of thy father, the God of Abraham, the God of Isaac, and the God of Jacob. And Moses hid his face; for he was afraid to look upon God. *Exodus 3:4-6*

EL SHADDAI - ALL ENCOMPASSING GOD - One who is more than enough, the all-sufficient One.

And when Abram was ninety years old and nine, the LORD appeared to Abram, and said unto him, I am the Almighty God; walk before me, and be thou perfect.

And I will make my covenant between me and thee, and will multiply thee exceedingly.   *Genesis 17:1,2*

JEHOVAH JIREH - MY PROVIDER - The God who has seen ahead and made provision for all my needs.

And Abraham lifted up his eyes, and looked, and behold behind him a ram caught in a thicket by his horns: and Abraham went and took the ram, and offered him up for a burnt offering in the stead of his son.

And Abraham called the name of that place **Jehovah-jireh**:
Genesis 22:13-14a

JEHOVAH M'KADDESH - MY SANCTIFIER - One who sets me apart from all others.

And that ye put on the new man, which after God is created in righteousness and true holiness. *Ephesians 4:24*

JEHOVAH NISSI - GOD MY BANNER - The God who makes me victorious.

And the LORD said unto Moses, Write this for a memorial in a book, and rehearse it in the ears of Joshua: for I will utterly put out the remembrance of Amalek from under heaven.

And Moses built an altar, and called the name of it **Jehovah-nissi:** *Exodus 17:14,15*

For the LORD your God is he that goeth with you, to fight for you against your enemies, to save you. *Deuteronomy 20:4*

He brought me to the banqueting house, and his banner over me was love. *Song of Solomon 2:4*

JEHOVAH ROPHE - MY HEALER - The God who heals.

If thou wilt diligently hearken to the voice of the LORD thy God, and wilt do that which is right in his sight, and wilt give ear to his commandments, and keep all his statutes, I will put none of these diseases upon thee, which I have brought upon the Egyptians: for **I am the Lord that healeth thee.**
Exodus 15:26

And the LORD will take away from thee all sickness, and will put none of the evil diseases of Egypt, which thou knowest, upon thee, but will lay them upon all them that hate thee.
Deuteronomy 7:15

JEHOVAH SHALOM - MY PEACE - God gives me abundant peace.

And the LORD said unto him, Peace be unto thee; fear not: thou shalt not die.

Then Gideon built an altar there unto the LORD, and called it **Jehovah-shalom**: *Judges 6:23, 24a*

I will both lay me down in peace, and sleep: for thou, LORD, only makest me dwell in safety. *Psalms 4:8*

JEHOVAH TSIDKENU - GOD MY RIGHTEOUSNESS - The Lord will be my righteousness.

Behold, the days come, saith the LORD, that I will raise unto David a righteous Branch, and a King shall reign and prosper, and shall execute judgment and justice in the earth.

In his days Judah shall be saved, and Israel shall dwell safely: and this is his name whereby he shall be called, **The Lord Our Righteousness.** *Jeremiah 23:5,6*

In those days shall Judah be saved, and Jerusalem shall dwell safely: and this is the name wherewith she shall be called, **The LORD our righteousness.** *Jeremiah 33:16*

JEHOVAH ROHI - GOD MY SHEPHERD - My intimate companion and friend.

And the LORD spake unto Moses face to face, as a man speaketh unto his friend. And he turned again into the camp: but his servant Joshua, the son of Nun, a young man, departed not out of the tabernacle. *Exodus 33:11*

The LORD is my shepherd; I shall not want. *Psalms 23:1*

Behold, the Lord GOD will come with strong hand, and his arm shall rule for him: behold, his reward is with him, and his work before him.

He shall feed his flock like a shepherd: he shall gather the lambs with his arm, and carry them in his bosom, and shall gently lead those that are with young. *Isaiah 40:10,11*

I am the good shepherd: the good shepherd giveth his life for the sheep. *John 10:11*

Now the God of peace, that brought again from the dead our Lord Jesus, that **great shepherd** of the sheep, through the blood of the everlasting covenant,

Make you perfect in every good work to do his will, working in you that which is wellpleasing in his sight, through Jesus Christ; to whom be glory for ever and ever. *Hebrews 13:20,21*

JEHOVAH SHAMMAH - GOD IS THERE - The presence of God goes with me everywhere.

And he said, My presence shall go with thee, and I will give thee rest. *Exodus 33:14*

It was round about eighteen thousand measures: and the name of the city from that day shall be, **The LORD is there.** *Ezekiel 48:35*

EL ELYON - THE MOST HIGH GOD - The Mighty One, Most High.

And Melchizedek king of Salem brought forth bread and wine: and he was the priest of the **most high God.**

And he blessed him, and said, Blessed be Abram of the **most high God,** possessor of heaven and earth:

And blessed be the **most high God,** which hath delivered thine enemies into thy hand. And he gave him tithes of all.

And the king of Sodom said unto Abram, Give me the persons, and take the goods to thyself.

And Abram said to the king of Sodom, I have lift up mine hand unto the LORD, the **most high God,** the possessor of heaven and earth, *Genesis 14:18-22*

JEHOVAH TSEBAOTH - THE LORD OF HOSTS - The God who will move the host of heaven to give me victory.

Then sang Deborah and Barak

Praise ye the **LORD** for the avenging of Israel, when the people willingly offered themselves.

So let all thine enemies perish, O LORD: but let them that love him be as the sun when he goeth forth in his might. And the land had rest forty years. *Judges 5:1a,2,31*

Bless ye the LORD, all ye his **hosts**; ye ministers of his, that do his pleasure. *Psalms 103:21*

JEHOVAH MAKKEH - THE LORD OUR SMITER - The God who chastens to perform His perfection in me.

Surely he hath borne our griefs, and carried our sorrows: yet we did esteem him stricken, smitten of God, and afflicted.

But he was wounded for our transgressions, he was bruised for our iniquities: the chastisement of our peace was upon him; and with his stripes we are healed.

Yet it pleased the LORD to bruise him; he hath put him to grief: when thou shalt make his soul an offering for sin, he shall see his seed, he shall prolong his days, and the pleasure of the LORD shall prosper in his hand. *Isaiah 53:4,5,10*

JEHOVAH GMOLAH - THE GOD OF RECOMPENSES
The God who compensates and rewards the choices we make.

To me belongeth vengeance, and **recompence**; their foot shall slide in due time: for the day of their calamity is at hand, and the things that shall come upon them make haste.

Deuteronomy 32:35

The **LORD recompense** thy work, and a full reward be given thee of the LORD God of Israel, under whose wings thou art come to trust. *Ruth 2:12*

Because the spoiler is come upon her, even upon Babylon, and her mighty men are taken, every one of their bows is broken: for the **LORD God of recompenses** shall surely requite.

Jeremiah 51:56

Dearly beloved, avenge not yourselves, but rather give place unto wrath: for it is written, Vengeance is mine; I will **repay,** saith the Lord. *Romans 12:19*

JEHOVAH ELONHAY - THE LORD MY GOD - The God who delivers me from trials.

And he said unto him, **Oh my Lord,** wherewith shall I save Israel? behold, my family is poor in Manasseh, and I am the least in my father's house. *Judges 6:15*

And Samson called unto the LORD, and said, **O Lord GOD,** remember me, I pray thee, and stregthen me, I pray thee, only this once, O God, that I may be at once avenged of the Philistines for my two eyes.
So the dead which he slew at his death were more than they which he slew in his life. *Judges 16:28,30b*

EL-ELOHE-ISRAEL - THE PERSONAL GOD OF ISRAEL
The personal God whom we can call to deliver others from fiery circumstances.

And Jacob asked him, and said, Tell me, I pray thee, thy name. And he said, Wherefore is it that thou dost ask after my name? And he blessed him there.

And Jacob called the name of the place Peniel: for I have seen God face to face, and my life is preserved.

And as he passed over Penuel the sun rose upon him, and he halted upon his thigh. *Genesis 32:29-31*

JEHOVAH ELOHEENU - THE LORD, OUR GOD - The God of the corporate Body of Christ.

And all the people brake off the golden earrings which were in their ears, and brought them unto Aaron.

And he received them at their hand, and fashioned it with a graving tool, after he had make it a molten calf: and they said, These be thy gods, O Israel, which brought thee up out of the land of Egypt.

And when Aaron saw it, he built an altar before it; and Aaron made proclamation, and said, Tomorrow is a feast to the **LORD**. *Exodus 32:3-5*

QUESTION

39 WHO IS JEUS?

For unto us a child is born, unto us a son is given: and the government shall be upon his shoulder: and his name shall be called Wonderful, Counsellor, The mighty God, The everlasting Father, The Prince of Peace. *Isaiah 9:6*

The book of the generation of Jesus Christ, the son of David, the son of Abraham.

And she shall bring forth a son, and thou shalt call his name JESUS: for he shall save his people from their sins.

Now all this was done, that it might be fulfilled which was spoken of the Lord by the prophet, saying,

Behold, a virgin shall be with child, and shall bring forth a son, and they shall call his name Emmanuel, which being interpreted is, God with us.   *Matthew 1:1,21-23*

For God so loved the world, that he gave his only begotten Son, that whosoever believeth in him should not perish, but have everlasting life.

For God sent not his Son into the world to condemn the world; but that the world through him might be saved.

John 3:16,17

Jesus saith unto him, I am the way, the truth, and the life: no man cometh unto the Father, but by me.   *John 14:6*

But these are written, that ye might believe that Jesus is the Christ, the Son of God; and that believing ye might have life through his name.   *John 20:31*

Be it known unto you all, and to all the people of Israel, that by the name of Jesus Christ of Nazareth, whom ye crucified, whom God raised from the dead, even by him doth this man stand here before you whole.

This is the stone which was set at nought of you builders, which is become the head of the corner.

Neither is there salvation in any other: for there is none other name under heaven given among men, whereby we must be saved.   *Acts 4:10-12*

For in him dwelleth all the fullness of the Godhead bodily. And ye are complete in him, which is the head of all principality and power: *Colossians 2:9,10*

Whosoever believeth that Jesus is the Christ is born of God: and every one that loveth him that begat loveth him also that is begotten of him.

He that hath the Son hath life; and he that hath not the Son of God hath no life.

These things have I written unto you that believe on the name of the Son of God; that ye may know that ye have eternal life, and that ye may believe on the name of the Son of God.

And we know that the Son of God is come, and hath given us an understanding, that we may know him that is true, and we are in him that is true, even in his Son Jesus Christ. This is true God, and eternal life. *1 John 5:1,12,13,20*

I Jesus have sent mine angel to testify unto you these things in the churches. I am the root and the offspring of David, and the bright and morning star. *Revelation 22:16*

QUESTION 40 IS JESUS THE ONLY WAY TO GET TO GOD?

Then said Jesus unto them again, Verily, verily, I say unto you, I am the door of the sheep.

I am the door: by me if any man enter in, he shall be saved, and shall go in and out, and find pasture.

I and my Father are one. *John 10:7,9,30*

Jesus saith unto him, I am the way, the truth, and the life: no man cometh unto the Father, but by me. *John 14:6*

Neither is there salvation in any other: for there is none other name under heaven given among men, whereby we must be saved.   *Acts 4:12*

For there is one God, and one mediator between God and men, the man Christ Jesus;   *I Timothy 2:5*

QUESTION
41 | WHAT DOES JESUS LOOK LIKE?

For he shall grow up before him as a tender plant, and as a root out of a dry ground: he hath no form nor comeliness; and when we shall see him, there is no beauty that we should desire him.

He is despised and rejected of men; a man of sorrows, and acquainted with grief: and we hid as it were our faces from him; he was despised, and we esteemed him not.   *Isaiah 53:2-3*

Behold my hands and my feet, that it is I myself: handle me, and see; for a spirit hath not flesh and bones, as ye see me have.   *Luke 24:39*

And in the midst of the seven candlesticks one like unto the Son of man, clothed with a garment down to the foot, and girt about the paps with a golden girdle.

His head and his hairs were white like wool, as white as snow; and his eyes were as a flame of fire;

And his feet like unto fine brass, as if they burned in a furnace; and his voice as the sound of many waters.

And he had in his right hand seven stars: and out of his mouth went a sharp twoedged sword: and his countenance was as the sun shineth in his strength.

And when I saw him, I fell at his feet as dead. And he laid his right hand upon me, saying unto me, Fear not; I am the first and the last: *Revelation 1:13-17b*

QUESTION 42 | WAS JESUS ACTUALLY GOD?

Behold, a virgin shall be with child, and shall bring forth a son, and they shall call his name Emmanuel, which being interpreted is, God with us. *Matthew 1:23*

In the beginning was the Word, and the Word was with God, and the Word was God.

All things were made by him; and without him was not any thing made that was made.

And the Word was made flesh, and dwelt among us, (and we beheld his glory, the glory as of the only begotten of the Father,) full of grace and truth.

The next day John seeth Jesus coming unto him, and saith, Behold the Lamb of God, which taketh away the sin of the world. *John 1:1,3,14,29*

Then answered Jesus and said unto them, Verily, verily, I say unto you, The Son can do nothing of himself, but what he seeth the Father do: for what things soever he doeth, these doeth the Son likewise.

For the Father loveth the Son, and sheweth him all things that himself doeth: and he will shew him greater works than these, that ye may marvel.

I can of mine own self do nothing: as I hear, I judge: and my judgment is just; because I seek not mine own will, but the will of the Father which hath sent me .

And the Father himself, which hath sent me, hath borne witness of me. Ye have neither heard his voice at any time, nor seen his shape. *John 5:19,20,30,37*

Jesus said unto them, Verily, verily, I say unto you, Before Abraham was, I am. *John 8:58*

My sheep hear my voice, and I know them, and they follow me:

And I give unto them eternal life; and they shall never perish, neither shall any man pluck them out of my hand.

My Father, which gave them me, is greater than all; and no man is able to pluck them out of my Father's hand.

I am my Father are one. *John 10:27-30*

For there is one God, and one mediator between God and men, the man Christ Jesus; *I Timothy 2:5*

And he is before all things, and by him all things consist. *Colossians 1:17*

For in him dwelleth all the fulness of the Godhead bodily.

And ye are complete in him, which is the head of all principality and power: *Colossians 2:9-10*

QUESTION 43 | WAS JESUS ACCEPTED BY THE MASSES?

And Jesus went about all Galilee, teaching in their synagogues, and preaching the gospel of the kingdom, and healing all manner of sickness and all manner of disease among the people.

And his fame went throughout all Syria: and they brought unto him all sick people that were taken with divers diseases and torments, and those which were possessed with devils, and those which were lunatick, and those that had the palsy; and he healed them.

And there followed him great multitudes of people from Galilee, and from Decapolis, and from Jerusalem, and from Judaea, and from beyond Jordan.   *Matthew 4:23-25*

But Jesus withdrew himself with his disciples to the sea: and a great multitude from Galilee followed him, and from Judaea,   *Mark 3:7*

And when they could not find by what way they might bring him in because of the multitude, they went upon the housetop, and let him down through the tiling with his couch into the midst before Jesus.   *Luke 5:19*

QUESTION 44 | WHO IS THE HOLY SPIRIT?

The Spirit of God hath made me, and the breath of the Almighty hath given me life.   *Job 33:4*

And it shall come to pass afterward, that I will pour out my spirit upon all flesh; and your sons and your daughters shall prophesy, your old men shall dream dreams, your young men shall see visions:

And also upon the servants and upon the handmaids in those days will I pour out my spirit.   *Joel 2:28-29*

But the Comforter, which is the Holy Ghost, whom the Father will send in my name, he shall teach you all things, and bring all things to your remembrance, whatsoever I have said unto you. *John 14:26*

But ye shall receive power, after that the Holy Ghost is come upon you: and ye shall be witnesses unto me both in Jerusalem, and in all Judaea, and in Samaria, and unto the uttermost part of the earth. *Acts 1:8*

And when the day of Pentecost was fully come, they were all with one accord in one place.

And suddenly there came a sound from heaven as of a rushing mighty wind, and it filled all the house where they were sitting.

And there appeared unto them cloven tongues like as of fire, and it sat upon each of them.

And they were filled with the Holy Ghost, and began to speak with other tongues, as the Spirit gave them utterance. *Acts 2:1-4*

This is he that came by water and blood, even Jesus Christ; not by water only, but by water and blood. And it is the Spirit that beareth witness, because the Spirit is truth.

For there are three that bear record in heaven, the Father, the Word, and the Holy Ghost: and these three are one. *I John 5:6,7*

QUESTION
45 HAS ANYONE EVER SEEN GOD?

And the LORD spake unto Moses face to face, as a man speaketh unto his friend.

And he said, thou canst not see my face: for there shall no man see me, and live.

And the LORD said, Behold, there is a place by me, and thou shalt stand upon a rock:

And it shall come to pass, while my glory passeth by, that I will put thee in a clift of the rock, and will cover thee with my hand while I pass by:

And I will take away mine hand, and thou shalt see my back parts: but my face shall not be seen.   *Exodus 33:11a, 20-23*

And they will tell it to the inhabitants of this land: for they have heard that thou LORD art among this people, that thou LORD art seen face to face, and that thy cloud standeth over them, and that thou goest before them, by day time in a pillar of a cloud, and in a pillar of fire by night.   *Numbers 14:14*

And there arose not a prophet since in Israel like unto Moses, whom the LORD knew face to face,   *Deuteronomy 34:10*

And he rode upon a cherub, and did fly: and he was seen upon the wings of the wind.   *II Samuel 22:11*

And I was as the colour of amber, as the appearance of fire round about within it, from the appearance of his loins even upward, and from the appearance of his loins even downward, I saw as it were the appearance of fire, and it had brightness round about.   *Ezekiel 1:27*

And the LORD shall be seen over them, and his arrow shall go forth as the lightning: and the Lord GOD shall blow the trumpet, and shall go with whirlwinds of the south.
      Zechariah 9:14

No man hath seen God at any time; the only begotten Son, which is in the bosom of the Father, he hath declared him.
      John 1:18

Which in his times he shall shew, who is the blessed and only Potentate, the King of kings, and Lord of lords;

Who only hath immortality, dwelling in the light which no man can approach unto; whom no man hath seen, nor can see: to whom be honour and power everlasting.   *I Timothy 6:15,16*

Behold, he cometh with clouds; and every eye shall see him, and they also which pierced him: and all kindreds of the earth shall wail because of him. Even so, Amen.   *Revelation 1:7*

QUESTION
46 | IS THERE MORE THAN ONE GOD?

The LORD he is God; there is none else beside him.
Deuteronomy 4:35b

Ye shall not go after other gods, of the gods of the people which are round about you;   *Deuteronomy 6:14*

I am the LORD, and there is none else, there is no God beside me: I girded thee, though thou hast not known me.

That they may know from the rising of the sun, and from the west, that there is none beside me, I am the LORD, and there is none else.

Tell ye, and bring them near; yea, let them take counsel together: who hath declared this from ancient time? have not I the LORD? and there is no God else beside me; a just God and a Saviour; there is none beside me.

Look unto me, and be ye saved, all the ends of the earth: for I am God, and there is none else.   *Isaiah 45:5-6, 21-22*

And Jesus answered him, The first of all the commandments is, Hear, O Israel; The Lord our God is one Lord:

And thou shalt love the Lord thy God with all thy heart, and with all thy soul, and with all thy mind, and with all thy strength: this is the first commandment.

And the second is like, namely this, Thou shalt love thy neighbour as thyself. There is none other commandment greater than these,

And the scribe said unto him, Well, Master, thou hast said the truth: for there is one God; and there is none other but he:
Mark 12:29-32

Seeing it is one God, which shall justify the circumcision by faith, and uncircumcision through faith.   *Romans 3:30*

Now a mediator is not a mediator of one, but God is one.
Galatians 3:20

There is one body, and one Spirit, even as ye are called in one hope of your calling;

One Lord, one faith, one baptism,

One God and Father of all, who is above all, and through all, and in you all.   *Ephesians 4:4-6*

For there is one God, and one mediator between God and men, the man Christ Jesus;   *I Timothy 2:5*

8

His Place

WHERE DOES GOD LIVE?

Howbeit the most High dwelleth not in temples made with hands; as saith the prophet,

Heaven is my throne, and earth is my footstool: what house will ye build me? saith the Lord: or what is the place of my rest?
Acts 7:48,49

God that made the world and all things therein, seeing that he is Lord of heaven and earth, dwelleth not in temples made with hands;
Acts 17:24

Know ye not that ye are the temple of God, and that the Spirit of God dwelleth in you?
I Corinthians 3:16

What? know ye not that he which is joined to an harlot is one body? for two, saith he, shall be one flesh.

What? know ye not that your body is the temple of the Holy Ghost which is in you, which ye have of God, and ye are not your own?
I Corinthians 6:16,19

And I heard a great voice out of heaven saying, Behold, the tabernacle of God is with men, and he will dwell with them, and they shall be his people, and God himself shall be with them, and be their God.

And I saw no temple therin: for the Lord God Almighty and the Lamb are the temple of it.
Revelation 21:3,22

QUESTION 48
WHAT DOES HEAVEN LOOK LIKE?

And he carried me away in the spirit to a great and high mountain, and shewed me that great city, the holy Jerusalem, descending out of heaven from God,

Having the glory of God: and her light was like unto a stone most precious, even like a jasper stone, clear as crystal;

And had a wall great and high, and had twelve gates, and at the gates twelve angels, and names written thereon, which are the names of the twelve tribes of the children of Israel:

On the east three gates; on the north three gates; on the south three gates; and on the west three gates.

And the wall of the city had twelve foundations, and in them the names of the twelve apostles of the Lamb.

And he that talked with me had a golden reed to measure the city, and the gates thereof, and the wall thereof.

And the city lieth foursquare, and the length is as large as the breadth: and he measured the city with the reed, twelve thousand furlongs. The length and the breadth and the height of it are equal.

And he measured the wall thereof, an hundred and forty and four cubits, according to the measure of a man, that is, of the angel.

And the building of the wall of it was of jasper: and the city was pure gold, like unto clear glass.

And the foundations of the wall of the city were garnished with all manner of precious stones. The first foundation was jasper; the second, sapphire; the third, a chalcedony; the fourth, an emerald;

The fifth, sardonyx; the sixth, sardius; the seventh, chrysolyte; the eighth, beryl; the ninth, a topaz; the tenth, a chrysoprasus; the eleventh, a jacinth; the twelfth, an amethyst.

And the twelve gates were twelve pearls: every several gate was of one pearl: and the street of the city was pure gold, as it were transparent glass.

And I saw no temple therein: for the Lord God Almighty and the Lamb are the temple of it.

And the city had no need of the sun, neither of the moon, to shine in it: for the glory of God did lighten it, and the Lamb is the light thereof.

And the nations of them which are saved shall walk in the light of it: and the kings of the earth do bring their glory and honour into it.

And the gates of it shall not be shut at all by day: for there shall be no night there. *Revelation 21:10-25*

And he shewed me a pure river of water of life, clear as crystal, proceeding out of the throne of God and of the Lamb.

In the midst of the street of it, and on either side of the river, was there the tree of life, which bare twelve manner of fruits, and yielded her fruit every month: and the leaves of the tree were for the healing of the nations.

And there shall be no more curse: but the throne of God and of the Lamb shall be in it; and his servants shall serve him:

And they shall see his face; and his name shall be in their foreheads.

And there shall be no night there; and they need no candle, neither light of the sun; for the Lord God giveth them light: and they shall reign for ever and ever. *Revelation 22:1-5*

QUESTION 49 | WHO SURROUNDS GOD IN HEAVEN?

Again he said, Therefore hear the word of the LORD; I saw the LORD sitting upon his throne, and all the host of heaven standing on his right hand and on his left. *II Chronicles 18:18*

And I beheld, and I heard the voice of many angels round about the throne and the beasts and the elders: and the number of them was ten thousand times ten thousand, and thousands of thousands;   *Revelation 5:11*

QUESTION 50 | DID GOD CREATE THE ANGELS?

Thou, even thou, art LORD alone; thou hast made heaven, the heaven of heavens, with all their host, the earth, and all things that are therein, the seas, and all that is therein, and thou preservest them all; and the host of heaven worshippeth thee.
Nehemiah 9:6

Who maketh his angels spirits; his ministers a flaming fire:
Psalms 104:4

The LORD hath made all things for himself: yea, even the wicked for the day of evil.   *Proverbs 16:4*

Lift up your eyes on high, and behold who hath created these things, that bringeth out their host by number: he calleth them all by names by the greatness of his might, for that he is strong in power; not one faileth.   *Isaiah 40:26*

Thou art worthy, O Lord, to receive glory and honour and power: for thou hast created all things, and for thy pleasure they are and were created.   *Revelation 4:11*

QUESTION 51 | WILL THERE BE MALES OR FEMALES IN HEAVEN?

The same day came to him the Sadducees, which say that there is no resurrection, and asked him,

Saying, Master, Moses said, If a man die, having no children, his brother shall marry his wife, and raise up seed unto his brother.

Now there were with us seven brethren: and the first, when he had married a wife, deceased, and, having no issue, left his wife, unto his brother:

Likewise the second also, and the third, unto the seventh.

And last of all the woman died also.

Therefore in the resurrection whose wife shall she be of the seven? for they all had her.

Jesus answered and said unto them, Ye do err, not knowing the scriptures, nor the power of God.

For in the resurrection they neither marry, nor are given in marriage, but are as the angels of God in heaven.

Matthew 22:23-30

For ye are all the children of God by faith in Christ Jesus.

There is neither Jew nor Greek, there is neither bond nor free, there is neither male nor female: for ye are all one in Christ Jesus. *Galatians 3:26,28*

Beloved, now are we the sons of God, and it doth not yet appear what we shall be: but we know that, when he shall appear, we shall be like him; for we shall see him as he is.

I John 3:2

QUESTION 52
HOW MANY ANGELS DOES GOD HAVE AROUND HIS THRONE?

And I beheld, and I heard the voice of many angels round about the throne and the beasts and the elders: and the number of them was ten thousand times ten thousand, and thousands of thousands;
Revelation 5:11

QUESTION 53
WHAT WAS GOD'S PURPOSE FOR ANGELS?

For he shall give his angels charge over thee, to keep thee in all thy ways.
Psalms 91:11

Bless the LORD, ye his angels, that excel in strength, that do his commandments, hearkening unto the voice of his word.
Psalms 103:20

And he shall send his angels with a great sound of a trumpet, and they shall gather together his elect from the four winds, from one end of heaven to the other.
Matthew 24:31

And he was there in the wilderness forty days, tempted of Satan; and was with the wild beasts; and the angels ministered unto him.
Mark 1:13

And it came to pass, that the beggar died, and was carried by the angels into Abraham's bosom: the rich man also died, and was buried;
Luke 16:22

And again, when he bringeth in the firstbegotten into the world, he saith, And let all the angels of God worship him.

And of the angels he saith, Who maketh his angels spirits, and his ministers a flame of fire.

But to which of the angels said he at any time, Sit on my right hand, until I make thine enemies thy footstool?

Hebrews 1:6,7,13

And there was war in heaven: Michael and his angels fought against the dragon; and the dragon fought and his angels,

Revelation 12:7

9
His Plans

QUESTION 54 — DOES GOD PLAN AHEAD?

For I know the thoughts that I think toward you, saith the LORD, thoughts of peace, and not of evil, to give you an expected end. *Jeremiah 29:11*

In my Father's house are many mansions: if it were not so, I would have told you. I go to prepare a place for you.

And if I go and prepare a place for you, I will come again, and receive you unto myself; that where I am, there ye may be also. *John 14:2-3*

QUESTION 55 — CAN GOD PREDICT THE FUTURE?

For the ways of man are before the eyes of the LORD, and he pondereth all his goings. *Proverbs 5:21*

Before I formed thee in the belly I knew thee; and before thou camest forth out of the womb I sanctified thee, and I ordained thee a prophet unto the nations. *Jeremiah 1:5*

Known unto God are all his works from the beginning of the world. *Acts 15:18*

And we know that all things work together for good to them that love God, to them who are the called according to his purpose.

For whom he did foreknow, he also did predestinate to be conformed to the image of his Son, that he might be the firstborn among many brethren.

Moreover whom he did predestinate, them he also called: and whom he called, them he also justified: and whom he justified, them he also glorified. *Romans 8:28-30*

Having predestinated us unto the adoption of children by Jesus Christ to himself, according to the good pleasure of his will,

In whom also we have obtained an inheritance, being predestinated according to the purpose of him who worketh all things after the counsel of his own will: *Ephesians 1:5,11*

QUESTION 56 WHY DID GOD GIVE US THE BIBLE?

This book of the law shall not depart out of thy mouth; but thou shalt meditate therein day and night, that thou mayest observe to do according to all that is written therein: for then thou shalt make thy way prosperous, and then thou shalt have good success. *Joshua 1:8*

Then shall I not be ashamed, when I have respect unto all thy commandments.

Wherewithal shall a young man cleanse his way? by taking heed thereto according to thy word.

With my whole heart have I sought thee: O let me not wander from thy commandments.

Thy word have I hid in mine heart, that I might not sin against thee.

My soul fainteth for thy salvation: but I hope in thy word.

Unless thy law had been my delights, I should then have perished in mine affliction.

Thou through thy commandments hast made me wiser than mine enemies: for they are ever with me.

I have more understanding than all my teachers: for thy testimonies are my meditation.

I understand more than the ancients, because I keep thy precepts.

How sweet are thy words unto my taste! yea, sweeter than honey to my mouth!

Through thy precepts I get understanding: therefore I hate every false way.

Thy word is a lamp unto my feet, and a light unto my path.

The entrance of thy words giveth light; it giveth understanding unto the simple.

Great peace have they which love thy law: and nothing shall offend them.

Psalms 119:6,9-11,81,92,98-100,103-105,130,165

My son, keep thy father's commandment, and forsake not the law of thy mother:

Bind them continually upon thine heart, and tie them about thy neck.

When thou goest, it shall lead thee; when thou sleepest, it shall keep thee; and when thou awakest, it shall talk with thee.

For the commandment is a lamp; and the law is light; and reproofs of instruction are the way of life: *Proverbs 6:20-23*

These things have I spoken unto you, that my joy might remain in you, and that your joy might be full.   *John 15:11*

All scripture is given by inspiration of God, and is profitable for doctrine, for reproof, for correction, for instruction in righteousness: *II Timothy 3:16*

For the prophecy came not in old time by the will of man: but holy men of God spake as they were moved by the Holy Ghost.   *II Peter 1:21*

57 HOW CAN I FIND THE WILL OF GOD FOR MY LIFE?

Wait on the LORD: be of good courage, and he shall strengthen thine heart: wait, I say, on the LORD. *Psalms 27:14*

I will instruct thee and teach thee in the way which thou shalt go: I will guide thee with mine eye.   *Psalms 32:8*

Ask, and it shall be given you; seek, and ye shall find; knock, and it shall be opened unto you:
For every one that asketh receiveth; and he that seeketh findeth; and to him that knocketh it shall be opened.
                                                            Matthew 7:7,8

Howbeit when he, the Spirit of truth, is come, he will guide you into all truth: for he shall not speak of himself; but whatsoever he shall hear, that shall he speak: and he will shew you things to come.   *John 16:13*

For as many as are led by the Spirit of God, they are the sons of God.   *Romans 8:14*

If any of you lack wisdom, let him ask of God, that giveth to all men liberally, and upbraideth not; and it shall be given him.
But let him ask in faith, nothing wavering. For he that wavereth is like a wave of the sea driven with the wind and tossed.   *James 1:5,6*

Draw nigh to God, and he will draw nigh to you.

James 4:8

10

His Power

QUESTION

58 | WILL GOD PERFORM MIRACLES TODAY?

Is any thing too hard for the LORD? At the time appointed I will return unto thee, according to the time of life, and Sarah shall have a son. *Genesis 18:14*

Behold, I am the LORD, the God of all flesh: is there any thing too hard for me? *Jeremiah 32:27*

Jesus said unto him, If thou canst believe, all things are possible to him that believeth. *Mark 9:23*

Jesus Christ the same yesterday, and to day, and for ever. *Hebrews 13:8*

And this is the confidence that we have in him, that, if we ask any thing according to his will, he heareth us:
And if we know that he hear us, whatsoever we ask, we know that we have the petitions that we desired of him. *I John 5:14,15*

QUESTION

59 | IS THERE ANYTHING GOD CANNOT DO?

Yea, they turned back and tempted God, and limited the Holy One of Israel. *Psalms 78:41*

Then came the word of the LORD unto Jeremiah, saying,
Behold, I am the LORD, the God of all flesh: is there any
thing too hard for me?   *Jeremiah 32:26,27*

And he did not many mighty works there because of their
unbelief.   *Matthew 13:58*

And he said, The things which are impossible with men are
possible with God.   *Luke 18:27*

11
His Power Over Demons

QUESTION
60 | HOW DO DEMONS REACT TO THE NAME OF JESUS?

And, behold, they cried out, saying, What have we to do with thee, Jesus, thou Son of God? art thou come hither to torment us before the time? *Matthew 8:29*

QUESTION
61 | WHO IS GOD'S CHIEF ADVERSARY?

How art thou fallen from heaven, O Lucifer, son of the morning! how art thou cut down to the ground, which didst weaken the nations!

For thou hast said in thine heart, I will ascend into heaven, I will exalt my throne above the stars of God: I will sit also upon the mount of the congregation, in the sides of the north:

I will ascend above the heights of the clouds; I will be like the most High.

Yet thou shalt be brought down to hell, to the sides of the pit. *Isaiah 14:12-15*

Be sober, be vigilant; because your adversary the devil, as a roaring lion, walketh about, seeking whom he may devour:

Whom resist steadfast in the faith, knowing that the same afflictions are accomplished in your brethren that are in the world. *I Peter 5:8-9*

And he laid hold on the dragon, that old serpent, which is the Devil, and Satan, and bound him a thousand years,

And cast him into the bottomless pit, and shut him up, and set a seal upon him, that he should deceive the nations no more, till the thousand years should be fulfilled: and after that he must be loosed a little season. *Revelation 20:2-3*

QUESTION 62 — WHAT IS GOD'S OPINION OF SATAN?

Ye are of your father the devil, and the lusts of your father ye will do. He was a murderer from the beginning, and abode not in the truth, because there is no truth in him. When he speaketh a lie, he speaketh of his own: for he is a liar, and the father of it. *John 8:44*

QUESTION 63 — WHAT WILL GOD EVENTUALLY DO WITH SATAN AND HIS DEMONS?

For God shall bring every work into judgment, with every secret thing, whether it be good, or whether it be evil.
Ecclesiastes 12:14

The Son of man shall send forth his angels, and they shall gather out of his kingdom all things that offend, and them which do iniquity;

And shall cast them into a furnace of fire: there shall be wailing and gnashing of teeth. *Matthew 13:41,42*

For if God spared not the angels that sinned, but cast them down to hell, and delivered them into chains of darkness, to be reserved unto judgment; *II Peter 2:4*

And the angels which kept not their first estate, but left their own habitation, he hath reserved in everlasting chains under darkness unto the judgment of the great day. *Jude 1:6*

And he laid hold on the dragon, that old serpent, which is the Devil, and Satan, and bound him a thousand years.

And cast him into the bottomless pit, and shut him up, and set a seal upon him, that he should deceive the nations no more, till the thousand years should be fulfilled: and after that he must be loosed a little season.

And when the thousand years are expired, Satan shall be loosed out of his prison, *Revelation 20:2,3,7*

12

His Power Over Sickness and Disease

WHAT IS GOD'S OPINION OF SICKNESS AND DISEASE?

And ye shall serve the LORD your God, and he shall bless thy bread, and thy water; and I will take sickness away from the midst of thee.   *Exodus 23:25*

And the LORD will take away from thee all sickness, and will put none of the evil diseases of Egypt, which thou knowest, upon thee; but will lay them upon all them that hate thee.
                                             Deuteronomy 7:15

The LORD will strengthen him upon the bed of languishing: thou wilt make all his bed in his sickness.
                                                    Psalms 41:3

Who forgiveth all thine iniquities; who healeth all thy diseases;   *Psalms 103:3*

He sent his word, and healed them, and delivered them from their destructions.   *Psalms 107:20*

For I will restore health unto thee, and I will heal thee of thy wounds, saith the Lord;   *Jeremiah 30:17a*

And Jesus saith unto him, I will come and heal him.

Matthew 8:7

They shall take up serpents; and if they drink any deadly thing, it shall not hurt them; they shall lay hands on the sick, and they shall recover. *Mark 16:18*

The thief cometh not, but for to steal, and to kill, and to destroy: I am come that they might have life, and that they might have it more abundantly. *John 10:10*

How God anointed Jesus of Nazareth with the Holy Ghost and with power: who went about doing good, and healing all that were oppressed of the devil; for God was with him.

Acts 10:38

Is any sick among you? let him call for the elders of the church; and let them pray over him, anointing him with oil in the name of the Lord:

And the prayer of faith shall save the sick, and the Lord shall raise him up; and if he have committed sins, they shall be forgiven him. *James 5:14,15*

Who his own self bare our sins in his own body on the tree, that we, being dead to sins, should live unto righteousness: by whose stripes ye were healed. *I Peter 2:24*

QUESTION 65
DOES GOD HAVE MORE THAN ONE METHOD FOR HEALING?

And when Elisha was come into the house, behold, the child was dead, and laid upon his bed.

He went in therefore, and shut the door upon them twain, and prayed unto the LORD.

And he went up, and lay upon the child, and put his mouth upon his mouth, and his eyes upon his eyes, and his hands upon his hands: and he stretched himself upon the child; and the flesh of the child waxed warm.

Then he returned, and walked in the house to and fro; and went up, and stretched himself upon him: and the child sneezed seven times, and the child opened his eyes.

And he called Gehazi, and said, Call this Shunammite. So he called her. And when she was come in unto him, he said, Take up thy son. *II Kings 4:32-36*

And Elisha sent a messenger unto him, saying, Go and wash in Jordan seven times, and thy flesh shall come again to thee, and thou shalt be clean. *II Kings 5:10*

He sent his word, and healed them, and delivered them from their destructions. *Psalms 107:20*

My son, attend to my words; incline thine ear unto my sayings.

Let them not depart from thine eyes; keep them in the midst of thine heart.

For they are life unto those that find them, and health to all their flesh. *Proverbs 4:20-22*

A merry heart doeth good like a medicine: but a broken spirit drieth the bones. *Proverbs 17:22*

For Isaiah had said, Let them take a lump of figs, and lay it for a plaister upon the boil, and he shall recover.   *Isaiah 38:21*

Surely he hath borne our griefs, and carried our sorrows: yet we did esteem him stricken, smitten of God, and afflicted.

But he was wounded for our transgressions, he was bruised for our iniquities: the chastisement of our peace was upon him; and with his stripes we are healed.   *Isaiah 53:4,5*

For I will restore health unto thee, and I will heal thee of thy wounds, saith the Lord;   *Jeremiah 30:17a*

And Jesus saith unto him, I will come and heal him.
                                                          Matthew 8:7

When he had thus spoken, he spat on the ground, and made clay of the spittle, and he anointed the eyes of the blind man with the clay,

And said unto him, Go, wash in the pool of Siloam, (which is by interpretation, Sent.)   He went his way therefore, and washed, and came seeing.   *John 9:6-7*

And God wrought special miracles by the hands of Paul:

So that from his body were brought unto the sick handkerchiefs or aprons, and diseases departed from them, and the evil spirits went out of them.   *Acts 19:11-12*

Is any among you afflicted? let him pray. Is any merry? let him sing psalms.

Is any sick among you? let him call for the elders of the church; and let them pray over him, anointing him with oil in the name of the Lord:

And prayer of faith shall save the sick, and the Lord shall raise him up; and if he have committed sins, they shall be forgiven him.

HIS POWER OVER SICKNESS AND DISEASE

Confess your faults one to another, and pray one for another, that ye may be healed. The effectual fervent prayer of a righteous man availeth much.   *James 5:13-16*

13

His Power To Forgive

WHY DID JESUS COME TO
THE EARTH?

And she shall bring forth a son, and thou shalt call his name
JESUS: for he shall save his people from their sins.

Matthew 1:21

Even as the Son of man came not to be ministered unto,
but to minister, and to give his life a ransom for many.

Matthew 20:28

And, behold, thou shalt conceive in thy womb, and bring
forth a son, and shalt call his name JESUS.

He shall be great, and shall be called the Son of the Highest:
and the Lord God shall give unto him the throne of his father
David:

And he shall reign over the house of Jacob for ever; and of
his kingdom there shall be no end.   *Luke 1:31-33*

For the Son of man is come to seek and to save that which
was lost.   *Luke 19:10*

For God so loved the world, that he gave his only begotten
Son, that whosoever believeth in him should not perish, but
have everlasting life.

For God sent not his Son into the world to condemn the
world; but that the world through him might be saved.

John 3:16,17

The thief cometh not, but for to steal, and to kill, and to destroy: I am come that they might have life, and that they might have it more abundantly. *John 10:10*

Christ hath redeemed us from the curse of the law, being made a curse for us: for it is written, Cursed is every one that hangeth on a tree:
That the blessing of Abraham might come on the Gentiles through Jesus Christ; that we might receive the promise of the Spirit through faith. *Galatians 3:13,14*

QUESTION 67 WHY IS THE BLOOD OF JESUS SO IMPORTANT TO GOD?

For this is my blood of the new testament, which is shed for many for the remission of sins. *Matthew 26:28*

Then Jesus said unto them, Verily, verily, I say unto you, Except ye eat the flesh of the Son of man, and drink his blood, ye have no life in you. *John 6:53*

For it is not possible that the blood of bulls and of goats should take away sins. *Hebrews 10:4*

Having therefore, brethren, boldness to enter into the holiest by the blood of Jesus, *Hebrews 10:19*

Now the God of peace, that brought again from the dead our Lord Jesus, that great shepherd of the sheep, through the blood of the everlasting covenant, *Hebrews 13:20*

Whom God hath set forth to be a propitiation through faith in his blood, to declare his righteousness for the remission of sins that are past, through the forbearance of God; *Romans 3:25*

In whom we have redemption through his blood, the forgiveness of sins, according to the riches of his grace;

Ephesians 1:7

And from Jesus Christ, who is the faithful witness, and the first begotten of the dead, and he prince of the kings of the earth. Unto him that loved us, and washed us from our sins in his own blood,

Revelation 1:5

QUESTION 68 | IS THERE ANY SIN GOD WILL NOT FORGIVE?

Verily I say unto you, All sins shall be forgiven unto the sons of men, and blasphemies wherewith soever they shall blaspheme:

But he that shall blaspheme against the Holy Ghost hath never forgiveness, but is in danger of eternal damnation:

Mark 3:28,29

QUESTION 69 | WHAT IS SIN TO GOD?

An high look, and a proud heart, and the plowing of the wicked, is sin.

Proverbs 21:4

The thought of foolishness is sin: and the scorner is an abomination to men.

Proverbs 24:9

And he that doubteth is damned if he eat, because he eateth not of faith: for whatsoever is not of faith is sin. *Romans 14:23*

Therefore to him that knoweth to do good, and doeth it not, to him it is sin.

James 4:17

Whosoever committeth sin transgresseth also the law: for sin is the transgression of the law.

He that committeth sin is of the devil; for the devil sinneth from the beginning. For this purpose the Son of God was manifested, that he might destroy the works of the devil.

I John 3:4,8

All unrighteousness is sin: and there is a sin not unto death.

I John 5:17

70 WHAT HAPPENS IF I DO NOT FORSAKE MY SINS?

For the wages of sin is death; but the gift of God is eternal life through Jesus Christ our Lord. *Romans 6:23*

And if Christ be in you, the body is dead because of sin; but the Spirit is life because of righteousness. *Romans 8:10*

The sting of death is sin; and the strength of sin is the law. *I Corinthians 15:56*

Whosoever committeth sin transgresseth also the law: for sin is the transgression of the law.

He that committeth sin is of the devil; for the devil sinneth from the beginning. For this purpose the Son of God was manifested, that he might destroy the works of the devil.

Whosoever is born of God doth not commit sin; for his seed remaineth in him: and he cannot sin, because he is born of God. *I John 3:4,8,9*

QUESTION 71 — WHAT HAPPENS TO MY SINS AFTER GOD FORGIVES ME?

As far as the east is from the west, so far hath he removed our transgressions from us.   *Psalms 103:12*

Behold, for peace I had great bitterness: but thou hast in love to my soul delivered it from the pit of corruption: for thou hast cast all my sins behind thy back.   *Isaiah 38:17*

I, even I, am he that blotteth out thy transgressions for mine own sake, and will not remember thy sins.   *Isaiah 43:25*

I have blotted out, as a thick cloud, thy transgressions, and, as a cloud, thy sins: return unto me; for I have redeemed thee.
Isaiah 44:22

And they shall teach no more every man his neighbour, and every man his brother, saying, Know the LORD: for they shall all know me, from the least of them unto the greatest of them, saith the LORD: for I will forgive their iniquity, and I will remember their sin no more.   *Jeremiah 31:34*

Who is a God like unto thee, that pardoneth iniquity, and passeth by the transgression of the remnant of his heritage? he retaineth not his anger for ever, because he delighteth in mercy.
He will turn again, he will have compassion upon us; he will subdue our iniquities; and thou wilt cast all their sins into the depths of the sea.   *Micah 7:18,19*

For I will be merciful to their unrighteousness, and their sins and their iniquities will I remember no more.
Hebrews 8:12

And their sins and iniquities will I remember no more.
Hebrews 10:17

QUESTION 72 — WHAT MUST I DO FOR GOD TO FORGIVE ALL MY SINS?

Whosoever therefore shall confess me before men, him will I confess also before my Father which is in heaven.

But whosoever shall deny me before men, him will I also deny before my Father which is in heaven.   *Matthew 10:32,33*

Him that cometh to me I will in no wise cast out.
John 6:37b

Believe on the Lord Jesus Christ, and thou shalt be saved, and thy house.   *Acts 16:31*

That if thou shalt confess with thy mouth the Lord Jesus, and shalt believe in thine heart that God hath raised him from the dead, thou shalt be saved.

For with the heart man believeth unto righteousness; and with the mouth confession is made unto salvation.
Romans 10:9,10

He that cometh to God must believe that he is, and that he is a rewarder of them that diligently seek him.   *Hebrews 11:6b*

If we confess our sins, he is faithful and just to forgive us our sins, and to cleanse us from all unrighteousness.   *I John 1:9*

His Praise

QUESTION 73

WHAT IS GOD'S OPINION OF SINGING?

And they sang together by course in praising and giving thanks unto the LORD; because he is good, for his mercy endureth for ever toward Israel.   *Ezra 3:11a*

I will praise the LORD according to his righteousness: and will sing praise to the name of the LORD most high.
                                                              Psalms 7:17

Sing praises to the LORD, which dwelleth in Zion: declare among the people his doings.   *Psalms 9:11*

Sing unto God, sing praises to his name: extol him that rideth upon the heavens by his name JAH, and rejoice before him.
Sing unto God, ye kingdoms of the earth; O sing praises unto the Lord; Selah: *Psalms 68:4,32*

I will praise the name of God with a song, and will magnify him with thanksgiving.   *Psalms 69:30*

It is a good thing to give thanks unto the LORD, and to sing praises unto thy name, O most High: *Psalms 92:1*

89

QUESTION 74 WHAT IS GOD'S OPINION OF MUSICAL INSTRUMENTS?

And it came to pass, when the evil spirit from God was upon Saul, that David took an harp, and played with his hand: so Saul was refreshed, and was well, and the evil spirit departed from him.   *I Samuel 16:23*

And with them Heman and Jeduthun with trumpets and cymbals for those that should make a sound, and with musical instruments of God. And the sons of Jeduthun were porters.
                                                    I Chronicles 16:42

Moreover four thousand were porters; and four thousand praised the LORD with the instruments which I made, said David, to praise therewith.   *I Chronicles 23:5*

And the priests waited on their offices: the Levites also with instruments of musick of the LORD, which David the king had made to praise the LORD, because his mercy endureth for ever, when David praised by their ministry; and the priests sounded trumpets before them, and all Israel stood.
                                                    II Chronicles 7:6

And the children of Israel that were present at Jerusalem kept the feast of unleavened bread seven days with great gladness: and the Levites and the priests praised the LORD day by day, singing with loud instruments unto the LORD.
                                                    II Chronicles 30:21

They take the timbrel and harp, and rejoice at the sound of the organ.   *Job 21:12*

Let them praise his name in the dance: let them sing praises unto him with the timbrel and harp. *Psalms 149:3*

Praise ye the LORD. Praise God in his sanctuary: praise him in the firmament of his power.

Praise him for his mighty acts: praise him according to his excellent greatness.

Praise him with the sound of the trumpet: praise him with the psaltery and harp.

Praise him with the timbrel and dance: praise him with stringed instruments and organs.

Praise him upon the loud cymbals: praise him upon the high sounding cymbals.

Let every thing that hath breath praise the LORD. Praise ye the LORD. *Psalms 150:1-6*

QUESTION 75 WHAT ARE GOD'S INSTRUCTIONS REGARDING PRAISE?

Speaking to yourselves in psalms and hymns and spiritual songs, singing and making melody in your heart to the Lord;

Giving thanks always for all things unto God and the Father in the name of our Lord Jesus Christ; *Ephesians 5:19-20*

Saying, I will declare thy name unto my brethren, in the midst of the church will I sing praise unto thee. *Hebrews 2:12*

I will therefore that men pray every where, lifting up holy hands, without wrath and doubting. *I Timothy 2:8*

QUESTION 76

WHO DOES GOD EXPECT TO WORSHIP AND PRAISE HIM?

Let the heaven and earth praise him, the seas, and everything that moveth therein. *Psalms 69:34*

Let everything that hath breath praise the LORD. Praise ye the LORD. *Psalms 150:6*

QUESTION 77

WHAT HAPPENS WHEN I PRAISE GOD?

And when he had consulted with the people, he appointed singers unto the LORD, and that should praise the beauty of holiness, as they went out before the army, and to say, Praise the LORD; for his mercy endureth for ever.

And when they began to sing and to praise, the LORD set ambushments against the children of Ammon, Moab, and mount Seir, which were come against Judah; and they were smitten. *II Chronicles 20:21,22*

Whoso offereth praise glorifieth me: and to him that ordereth his conversation aright will I shew the salvation of God. *Psalms 50:23*

QUESTION 78 | HOW CAN MAN GLORIFY AND EXPRESS PRAISE TO GOD?

Give unto the LORD the glory due unto his name: bring an offering, and come before him: worship the LORD in the beauty of holiness. *I Chronicles 16:29*

I will praise the LORD according to his righteousness: and will sing praise to the name of the LORD most high.
Psalms 7:17

O clap your hands, all ye people; shout unto God with the voice of triumph. *Psalms 47:1*

O come, let us worship and bow down: let us kneel before the LORD our maker. *Psalms 95:6*

Make a joyful noice unto the LORD, all ye lands.
Serve the LORD with gladness: come before his presence with singing.
Enter into his gates with thanksgiving, and into his courts with praise: be thankful unto him, and bless his name.
Psalms 100:1,2,4

Let them praise his name in the dance: let them sing praises unto him with the timbrel and harp. *Psalms 149:3*

Praise him with the timbrel and dance: praise him with stringed instruments and organs. *Psalms 150:4*

I will therefore that men pray every where, lifting up holy hands, without wrath and doubting. *I Timothy 2:8*

15

His Preachers, Pastors, and Priests

QUESTION
79 WHAT DOES GOD CALL THE MEN AND WOMEN WHO REPRESENT HIS MESSAGE ON EARTH?

But ye shall be named the Priests of the LORD: men shall call you the Ministers of our God: ye shall eat the riches of the Gentiles, and in their glory shall ye boast yourselves.

Isaiah 61:6

Ye are my friends, if ye do whatsoever I command you.

Henceforth I call you not servants; for the servant knoweth not what his lord doeth: but I have called you friends; for all things that I have heard of my Father I have made known unto you.

Ye have not chosen me, but I have chosen you, and ordained you, that ye should go and bring forth fruit, and that your fruit should remain: that whatsoever ye shall ask of the Father in my name, he may give it to you. *John 15:14-16*

And on my servants and on my handmaidens I will pour out in those days of my Spirit; and they shall prophesy:

Acts 2:18

Unto the church of God which is at Corinth, to them that are sanctified in Christ Jesus, called to be saints, with all that in every place call upon the name of Jesus Christ our Lord, both theirs and ours. *I Corinthians 1:2*

Who then is Paul, and who is Apollos, but ministers by whom ye believed, even as the Lord gave to every man?

I Corinthians 3:5

Let a man so account of us, as of the ministers of Christ, and stewards of the mysteries of God.   *I Corinthians 4:1*

Who also hath made us able ministers of the new testament; not of the letter, but of the spirit: for the letter killeth, but the spirit giveth life.   *II Corinthians 3:6*

Now then we are ambassadors for Christ, as though God did beseech you by us: we pray you in Christ's stead, be ye reconciled to God.   *II Corinthians 5:20*

And of the angels he saith, Who maketh his angels spirits, and his ministers a flame of fire.   *Hebrews 1:7*

The Revelation of Jesus Christ, which God gave unto him, to shew unto his servants things which must shortly come to pass; and he sent and signified it by his angel unto his servant John:
And hath made us kings and priests unto God

Revelation 1:1,6a

QUESTION 80 WHAT ARE THE MAJOR CATEGORIES AND TYPES OF MINISTERS?

And he gave some, apostles; and some, prophets; and some, evangelists; and some, pastors and teachers;
For the perfecting of the saints, for the work of the ministry, for the edifying of the body of Christ: *Ephesians 4:11-12*

QUESTION 81

WHAT ARE THE MINISTERS OF GOD PLACED ON EARTH TO DO?

The spirit of the Lord GOD is upon me; because the LORD hath anointed me to preach good tidings unto the meek; he hath sent me to bind up the brokenhearted, to proclaim liberty to the captives, and the opening of the prison to them that are bound;

To proclaim the acceptable year of the LORD, and the day of vengeance of our God; to comfort all that mourn;

To appoint unto them that mourn in Zion, to give unto them beauty for ashes, the oil of joy for mourning, the garment of praise for the spirit of heaviness; that they might be called trees of righteousness, the planting of the LORD, that he might be glorified.

And they shall build the old wastes, they shall raise up the former desolations, and they shall repair the waste cities, the desolations of many generations.

But ye shall be named the Priests of the LORD: men shall call you the Ministers of our God: ye shall eat the riches of the Gentiles, and in their glory shall ye boast yourselves.

Isaiah 61:1-4,6

And as ye go, preach, saying, The kingdom of heaven is at hand.

Heal the sick, cleanse the lepers, raise the dead, cast out devils: freely ye have received, freely give.   *Matthew 10:7,8*

What I tell you in darkness, that speak ye in light: and what ye hear in the ear, that preach ye upon the housetops.

Matthew 10:27

And he said unto them, Go ye into all the world, and preach the gospel to every creature.

He that believeth and is baptized shall be saved; but he that believeth not shall be damned.

And these signs shall follow them that believe; In my name shall they cast out devils; they shall speak with new tongues;

They shall take up serpents; and if they drink any deadly thing, it shall not hurt them; they shall lay hands on the sick, and they shall recover.   *Mark 16:15-18*

And he sent them to preach the kingdom of God, and to heal the sick.   *Luke 9:2*

Jesus said unto him, Let the dead bury their dead: but go thou and preach the kingdom of God.   *Luke 9:60*

Ye have not chosen me, but I have chosen you, and ordained you, that ye should go and bring forth fruit, and that your fruit should remain: that whatsoever ye shall ask of the Father in my name, he may give it to you.   *John 15:16*

How then shall they call on him in whom they have not believed? and how shall they believe in him of whom they have not heard? and how shall they hear without a preacher?
                                        Romans 10:14

Preach the word; be instant in season, out of season; reprove, rebuke, exhort with all longsuffering and doctrine.
                                        II Timothy 4:2

16

His Presence

QUESTION
82

IS IT POSSIBLE TO FEEL THE PRESENCE OF GOD?

And he said, My presence shall go with thee, and I will give thee rest.   *Exodus 33:14*

Whither shall I go from thy spirit? or whither shall I flee from thy presence?   *Psalms 139:7*

And when they had prayed, the place was shaken where they were assembled together; and they were all filled with the Holy Ghost, and they spake the word of God with boldness.
Acts 4:31

And the disciples were filled with joy, and with the Holy Ghost.   *Acts 13:52*

The Spirit itself beareth witness with our spirit, that we are the children of God: *Romans 8:16*

QUESTION
83

HOW DO I KNOW THAT GOD EXISTS?

The heavens declare the glory of God; and the firmament sheweth his handiwork.

Day unto day uttereth speech, and night unto night sheweth knowledge.

There is no speech nor language, where their voice is not heard.

Their line is gone out through all the earth, and their words to the end of the world. In them hath he set a tabernacle for the sun,

Which is as a bridegroom coming out of his chamber, and rejoiceth as a strong man to run a race.

His going forth is from the end of the heaven, and his circuit unto the ends of it: and there is nothing hid from the heat thereof.   *Psalms 19:1-6*

My sheep hear my voice, and I know them, and they follow me: *John 10:27*

For the invisible things of him from the creation of the world are clearly seen, being understood by the things that are made, even his eternal power and Godhead; so that they are without excuse: *Romans 1:20*

The Spirit itself beareth witness with our spirit, that we are the children of God: *Romans 8:16*

No man hath seen God at any time. If we love one another, God dwelleth in us, and his love is perfected in us.

Hereby know we that we dwell in him, and he in us, because he hath given us of his Spirit.   *I John 4:12*

QUESTION 84 CAN GOD BE EVERYWHERE AT THE SAME TIME?

And, behold, I am with thee, and will keep thee in all places whither thou goest, and will bring thee again into this land; for I will not leave thee, until I have done that which I have spoken to thee of.

And Jacob awaked out of his sleep, and he said, Surely the LORD is in this place; and I knew it not.

And he was afraid, and said, How dreadful is this place! this is none other but the house of God, and this is the gate of heaven.   *Genesis 28:15-17*

The earth is full of the goodness of the LORD. *Psalms 33:5b*

Whither shall I go from thy spirit? or whither shall I flee from thy presence?

If I ascent up into heaven, thou art there: if I make my bed in hell, behold, thou art there.

If I take the wings of the morning, and dwell in the uttermost parts of the sea;   *Psalms 139:7-9*

The eyes of the LORD are in every place, beholding the evil and the good.   *Proverbs 15:3*

Am I a God at hand, saith the LORD, and not a God afar off?

Can any hide himself in secret places that I shall not see him? saith the LORD. Do not I fill heaven and earth? saith the LORD.   *Jeremiah 23:23,24*

I will never leave thee, nor forsake thee.   *Hebrews 13:5b*

QUESTION 85 WHO DID GOD SENT TO MAN AFTER JESUS RETURNED TO HEAVEN?

And I will pray the Father, and he shall give you another Comforter, that he may abide with you for ever;

I will not leave you comfortless: I will come to you.

But the Comforter, which is the Holy Ghost, whom the Father will send in my name, he shall teach you all things, and bring all things to your remembrance, whatsoever I have said unto you.

Peace I leave with you, my peace I give unto you: not as the world giveth, give I unto you. Let not your heart be troubled, neither let it be afraid.

But that the world may know that I love the Father; and as the Father gave me commandment, even so I do. Arise, let us go hence.   *John 14:16,18,26,27,31*

Nevertheless I tell you the truth; It is expedient for you that I go away: for if I go not away, the Conforter will not come unto you; but if I depart, I will send him unto you.   *John 16:7*

For John truly baptized with water; but ye shall be baptized with the Holy Ghost not many days hence.

But ye shall receive power, after that the Holy Ghost is come upon you: and ye shall be witnesses unto me both in Jerusalem, and in all Judaea, and in Samaria, and unto the uttermost part of the earth.   *Acts 1:5,8*

And they were all filled with the Holy Ghost, and began to speak with other tongues, as the Spirit gave them utterance.

Therefore being by the right hand of God exalted, and having received of the Father the promise of the Holy Ghost, he hath shed forth this, which ye now see and hear.

Then Peter said unto them, Repent, and he baptized every one of you in the name of Jesus Christ for the remission of sins, and ye shall receive the gift of the Holy Ghost.   *Acts 2:4,33,38*

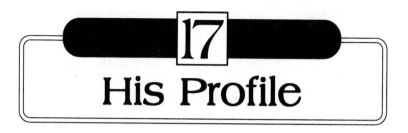

His Profile

86 | WHAT DOES GOD'S VOICE SOUND LIKE?

And after the earthquake a fire; but the LORD was not in the fire: and after the fire a still small voice.

And it was so, when Elijah heard it that he wrapped his face in his mantle, and went out, and stood in the entering in of the cave. And, behold, there came a voice unto him, and said, What doest thou here, Elijah?   *I Kings 19:12,13*

The voice of the LORD is upon the waters: the God of glory thundereth: the LORD is upon many waters.

The voice of the LORD breaketh the cedars; yea, the LORD breaketh the cedars of Lebanon.

The voice of the LORD divideth the flames of fire.
                                                     Psalms 29;3,5,7

And his feet like unto fine brass, as if they burned in a furnace; and his voice as the sound of many waters.
                                                     Revelation 1:15

And I heard a voice from heaven, as the voice of many waters, and as the voice of a great thunder: and I heard the voice of harpers harping with their harps: *Revelation 14:2*

QUESTION 87 | WHAT DOES GOD LOOK LIKE?

And God said, Let us make man in our image, after our likeness: *Genesis 1:26a*

For in the image of God made he man.   *Genesis 9:6b*

As the appearance of the bow that is in the cloud in the day of rain, so was the appearance of the brightness round about. This was the appearance of the likeness of the glory of the LORD. And when I saw it, I fell upon my face, and I heard a voice of one that spake.   *Ezekiel 1:28*

Then I beheld, and lo a likeness as the appearance of fire: from the appearance of his loins even downward, fire; and from his loins even upward, as the appearance of brightness, as the colour of amber.   *Ezekiel 8:2*

I beheld till the thrones were cast down, and the Ancient of days did sit, whose garment was white as snow, and the hair of his head like the pure wool: *Daniel 7:9a*

And the Word was made flesh, and dwelt among us, (and we beheld his glory, the glory as of the only begotten of the Father,) full of grace and truth.   *John 1:14*

QUESTION 88

WHAT COLOR OR RACE IS GOD?

Forasmuch then as we are the offspring of God, we ought not to think that the Godhead is like unto gold, or silver, or stone, graven by art and man's device.   *Acts 17:29*

Is he the God of the Jews only? Is he not also of the Gentiles? Yes, of the Gentiles also: *Romans 3:29*

For there is no difference between the Jew and the Greek: for the same Lord over all is rich unto all that call upon him.
Romans 10:12

There is neither Jew nor Greek, there is neither bond nor free, there is neither male nor female: for ye are all one in Christ Jesus.   *Galatians 3:28*

QUESTION 89

IS GOD MALE OR FEMALE?

To whom will ye liken me, and make me equal, and compare me, that we may be like?
Remember the former things of old: for I am God, and there is none else; I am God, and there is none like me,
Isaiah 46:5,9

God is a Spirit: and they that worship him must worship him in spirit and in truth.   *John 4:24*

90 DOES GOD SLEEP?

Behold, he that keepeth Israel shall neither slumber nor sleep.
Psalms 121:4

QUESTION

91 IS GOD MARRIED?

Turn, O backsliding children, saith the LORD; for I am married unto you: and I will take you one of a city, and two of a family, and I will bring you to Zion:

Surely as a wife treacherously departeth from her husband, so have ye dealt treacherously with me, O house of Israel, saith the LORD. *Jeremiah 3:14,20*

Let us be glad and rejoice, and give honour to him: for the marriage of the Lamb is come, and his wife hath made herself ready. *Revelation 19:7*

And I John saw the holy city, new Jerusalem, coming down from God out of heaven, prepared as a bride adorned for her husband.

And there came unto me one of the seven angels which had the seven vials full of the seven last plagues, and talked with me, saying, Come hither, I will shew thee the bride, the Lamb's wife. *Revelation 21:2,9*

And the Spirit and the bride say, Come. And let him that heareth say, Come. And let him that is athirst come. And whosoever will, let him take the water of life freely,

Revelation 22:17

QUESTION 92

HOW DOES THE BIBLE DESCRIBE THE CHARACTER AND NATURE OF GOD?

God is not a man, that he should lie; neither the son of man, that he should repent: hath he said, and shall he not do it? or hath he spoken, and shall he not make it good?

Numbers 23:19

The heavens declare his righteousness, and all the people see his glory.   *Psalms 97:6*

Great is our Lord, and of great power: his understanding is infinite.   *Psalms 147:5*

And one cried unto another, and said, Holy, holy, holy, is the LORD of hosts: the whole earth is full of his glory.

Isaiah 6:3

The Lord is slow to anger, and great in power, and will not at all acquit the wicked: the Lord hath his way in the whirlwind and in the storm, and the clouds are the dust of his feet.

Nahum 1:3

But God, who is rich in mercy, for his great love wherewith he loved us,   *Ephesians 2:4*

For we know him that hath said, Vengeance belongeth unto me, I will recompense, saith the Lord.   *Hebrews 10:30a*

This then is the message which we have heard of him, and declare unto you, that God is light, and in him is no darkness at all.   *I John 1:5*

Beloved, let us love one another: for love is of God; and every one that loveth is born of God, and knoweth God.

He that loveth not knoweth not God; for God is love.

Herein is love, not that we loved God, but that he loved us, and sent his Son to be the propitiation for our sins.

If we love one another, God dwelleth in us, and his love is perfected in us.

God is love; and he that dwelleth in love dwelleth in God, and God in him.   *I John 4:7-8,10,12b,16b*

QUESTION 93 HOW DOES THE IMPERFECTION OF MAN COMPARE TO THE PERFECTION OF GOD?

Sanctify yourselves therefore, and be ye holy: for I am the LORD your God.   *Leviticus 20:7*

For the LORD seeth not as man seeth; for man looketh on the outward appearance, but the LORD looketh on the heart.   *I Samuel 16:7b*

As for God, his way is perfect; the word of the LORD is tried: he is a buckler to all them that trust in him.   *II Samuel 22:31*

Out of Zion, the perfection of beauty, God hath shined.   *Psalms 50:2*

To whom then will ye liken God? or what likeness will ye compare unto him?   *Isaiah 40:18*

But we are all as an unclean thing, and all our righteousnesses are as filthy rags; and we all do fade as a leaf; and our iniquities, like the wind, have taken us away.   *Isaiah 64:6*

Be ye therefore perfect, even as your Father which is in heaven is perfect.   *Matthew 5:48*

As it is written, There is none righteous, no, not one:
For all have sinned, and come short of the glory of God;
                                                    Romans 3:10,23

But as he which hath called you is holy, so be ye holy in all manner of conversation;
Because it is written, Be ye holy; for I am holy.
                                                    I Peter 1:15,16

QUESTION 94 — DOES GOD HAVE NUMBERS THAT ARE SPECIAL OR SIGNIFICANT?

SEVEN

And on the seventh day God ended his work which he had made; and he rested on the seventh day from all his work which he had made.

And God blessed the seventh day, and sanctified it: because that in it he had rested from all his work which God created and made.   *Genesis 2:2,3*

Seven times a day do I praise thee because of thy righteous judgments.   *Psalms 119:164*

And here is the mind which hath wisdom. The seven heads are seven mountains, on which the woman sitteth.

And there are seven kings: five are fallen, and one is, and the other is not yet come; and when he cometh, he must continue a short space.

And the beast that was, and is not, even he is the eighth, and is of the seven, and goeth into perdition.
                                                    Revelation 17:9-11

TEN

After this I saw in the night visions, and behold a fourth beast, dreadful and terrible, and strong exceedingly; and it had great iron teeth: it devoured and brake in pieces, and stamped the residue with the feet of it: and it was diverse from all the beasts that were before it; and it had ten horns.   *Daniel 7:7*

And the ten horns which thou sawest are ten kings, which have received no kingdom as yet; but receive power as kings one hour with the beast.   *Revelation 17:12*

TWELVE

And Moses wrote all the words of the LORD, and rose up early in the morning, and builded an altar under the hill, and twelve pillars, according to the twelve tribes of Israel.
    Exodus 24:4

And thou shalt make the breastplate of judgment with cunning work; after the work of the ephod thou shalt make it; of gold, of blue, and of purple, and of scarlet, and of fine twined linen, shalt thou make it.   *Exodus 28:15*

Now the names of the twelve apostles are these; The first, Simon, who is called Peter, and Andrew his brother; James the son of Zebedee, and John his brother;
    Philip, and Bartholomew; Thomas, and Matthew the publican; James the son of Alphaeus, and Lebbaeus, whose surname was Thaddaeus;
    Simon the Canaanite, and Judas Iscariot, who also betrayed him.
    These twelve Jesus sent forth, and commanded them, saying, Go not into the way of the Gentiles, and into any city of the Samaritans enter ye not: *Matthew 10:2-5*

And he measured the wall thereof, an hundred and forty and four cubits, according to the measure of a man, that is, of the angel.

And the twelve gates were twelve pearls: every several gate was of one pearl: and the street of the city was pure gold, as it were transparent glass.   *Revelation 21:17,21*

In the midst of the street of it, and on either side of the river, was there the tree of life, which bare twelve manner of fruits, and yielded her fruit every month: and the leaves of the tree were for the healing of the nations.   *Revelation 22:2*

FORTY

And Moses went into the midst of the cloud, and gat him up into the mount: and Moses was in the mount forty days and forty nights.   *Exodus 24:18*

And Jonah began to enter into the city a day's journey, and he cried, and said, Yet forty days, and Nineveh shall be overthrown.   *Jonah 3:4*

And Jesus being full of the Holy Ghost returned from Jordan, and was led by the Spirit into the wilderness,

Being forty days tempted of the devil. And in those days he did eat nothing: and when they were ended, he afterward hungered.   *Luke 4;1,2*

FIFTY

And ye shall hallow the fiftieth year, and proclaim liberty throughout all the land unto all the inhabitants thereof: it shall be a jubilee unto you; and ye shall return every man unto his possession, and ye shall return every man unto his family.

Leviticus 25:10

ONE HUNDRED

Then Isaac sowed in that land, and received in the same year an hundredfold: and the LORD blessed him.

Genesis 26:12

And five of you shall chase an hundred, and an hundred of you shall put ten thousand to flight: *Leviticus 26:8a*

And Joab said unto the king, Now the LORD thy God add unto the people, how many soever they be, an hundredfold, and that the eyes of my lord the king may see it: but why doth my lord the king delight in this thing? *II Samuel 24:3*

TEN THOUSAND

And five of you shall chase an hundred, and an hundred of you shall put ten thousand to flight: and your enemies shall fall before you by the sword. *Leviticus 26:8*

How should one chase a thousand, and two put ten thousand to flight, except their Rock had sold them, and the LORD had shut them up? *Deuteronomy 32:30*

A thousand shall fall at thy side, and ten thousand at thy right hand; but it shall not come nigh thee. *Psalms 91:7*

QUESTION

95 WILL GOD EVER DIE?

But the Lord shall endure for ever: *Psalms 9:7a*

But thou, O Lord, shalt endure for ever; and thy remembrance unto all generations.

I said, O my God, take me not away in the midst of my days: thy years are throughout all generations.

But thou art the same, and thy years shall have no end.

Psalms 102:12,24,27

And, Thou, Lord, in the beginning hast laid the foundation of the earth; and the heavens are the works of thine hands:

They shall perish; but thou remainest; and they all shall wax old as doth a garment;

And as a vesture shalt thou fold them up, and they shall be changed: but thou art the same, and thy years shall not fail.

Hebrews 1:10-12

Without father, without mother, without descent, having neither beginning of days, nor end of life; but made like unto the Son of God; abideth a priest continually.   *Hebrews 7:3*

Being born again, not of corruptible seed, but of incorruptible, by the word of God, which liveth and abideth for ever.   *I Peter 1:23*

His Promises

QUESTION 96 WHAT ARE GOD'S PROMISES TO THOSE WHO TITHE AND GIVE OFFERINGS?

Then Isaac sowed in that land, and received in the same year an hundredfold: and the LORD blessed him.

And the man waxed great, and went forward, and grew until he became very great:

For he had possession of flocks, and possession of herds, and great store of servants: and the Philistines envied him.

Genesis 26:12-14

Honour the Lord with thy substance, and with the firstfruits of all thine increase:

So shall thy barns be filled with plenty, and thy presses shall burst out with new wine. *Proverbs 3:9,10*

There is that scattereth, and yet increaseth; and there is that withholdeth more than is meet, but it tendeth to poverty.

The liberal soul shall be made fat: and he that watereth shall be watered also himself.

He that withholdeth corn, the people shall curse him: but blessing shall be upon the head of him that selleth it.

Proverbs 11:24-26

He that hath a bountiful eye shall be blessed; for he giveth of his bread to the poor. *Proverbs 22:9*

Cast thy bread upon the waters: for thou shalt find it after many days. *Ecclesiastes 11:1*

Bring ye all the tithes into the storehouse, that there may be meat in mine house, and prove me now herewith, saith the LORD of hosts, if I will not open you the windows of heaven, and pour you out a blessing, that there shall not be room enough to receive it.

And I will rebuke the devourer for your sakes, and he shall not destroy the fruits of your ground; neither shall your vine cast her fruit before the time in the field, saith the LORD of hosts.

And all nations shall call you blessed: for ye shall be a delightsome land, saith the LORD of hosts. *Malachi 3:10-12*

Give, and it shall be given unto you; good measure, pressed down, and shaken together, and running over, shall men give into your bosom. For with the same measure that ye mete withal it shall be measured to you again. *Luke 6:38*

Upon the first day of the week let every one of you lay by him in store, as God hath prospered him, that there be no gatherings when I come. *I Corinthians 16:2*

QUESTION 97 — WHAT ARE GOD'S PROMISES TO THOSE WHO ARE SICK AND AFFLICTED?

And said, If thou wilt diligently hearken to the voice of the LORD thy God, and wilt do that which is right in his sight, and wilt give ear to his commandments, and keep all his statutes, I will put none of these diseases upon thee, which I have brought upon the Egyptians: for I am the LORD that healeth thee.
Exodus 15:26

And the LORD will take away from thee all sickness, and will put none of the evil diseases of Egypt, which thou knowest, upon thee; but will lay them upon all them that hate thee.

Deuteronomy 7:15

Bless the LORD, O my soul, and forget not all his benefits:

Who forgiveth all thine iniquities; who healeth all thy diseases;

Who redeemeth thy life from destruction; who crowneth thee with lovingkindness and tender mercies;

Who satisfieth thy mouth with good things; so that thy youth is renewed like the eagle's. *Psalms 103:2-5*

He sent his word, and healed them, and delivered them from their destructions. *Psalms 107:20*

My son, attend to my words; incline thine ear unto my sayings.

For they are life unto those that find them, and health to all their flesh. *Proverbs 4:20,22*

A merry heart doeth good like a medicine: but a broken spirit drieth the bones. *Proverbs 17:22*

Surely he hath borne our griefs, and carried our sorrows: yet we did esteem him stricken, smitten of God, and afflicted.

But he was wounded for our transgressions, he was bruised for our iniquities: the chastisement of our peace was upon him; and with his stripes we are healed. *Isaiah 53:4,5*

For I will restore health unto thee, and I will heal thee of thy wounds, saith the LORD; *Jeremiah 30:17a*

And Jesus saith unto him, I will come and heal him.

Matthew 8:7

How God anointed Jesus of Nazareth with the Holy Ghost and with power: who went about doing good, and healing all that were oppressed of the devil; for God was with him.

Acts 10:38

Who his own self bare our sins in his own body on the tree, that we, being dead to sins, should live unto righteousness: by whose stripes ye were healed. *I Peter 2:24*

Is any among you afflicted? let him pray. Is any merry? let him sing psalms.

Is any sick among you? let him call for the elders of the church; and let them pray over him, anointing him with oil in the name of the Lord:

And the prayer of faith shall save the sick, and the Lord shall raise him up; and if he have committed sins, they shall be forgiven him.

Confess your faults one to another, and pray one for another, that ye may be healed. The effectual fervent prayer of a righteous man availeth much. *James 5:13-16*

QUESTION 98 — WHAT ARE GOD'S PROMISES TO THOSE WHO HELP THE POOR?

He that hath pity upon the poor lendeth unto the LORD; and that which he hath given will he pay him again.

Proverbs 19:17

He that hath a bountiful eye shall be blessed; for he giveth of his bread to the poor. *Proverbs 22:9*

He that giveth unto the poor shall not lack: but he that hideth his eyes shall have many a curse. *Proverbs 28:27*

Give, and it shall be given unto you; good measure, pressed down, and shaken together, and running over, shall men give into your bosom. For with the same measure that ye mete withal it shall be measured to you again.   *Luke 6:38*

But whoso hath this world's good, and seeth his brother have need, and shutteth up his bowels of compassion from him, how dwelleth the love of God in him?

My little children, let us not love in word, neither in tongue; but in deed and in truth.   *I John 3:17,18*

QUESTION 99
WHAT ARE GOD'S PROMISED REWARDS TO THOSE WHO OBEY HIM?

If ye be willing and obedient, ye shall eat the good of the land: *Isaiah 1:19*

Blessed is the man that endureth temptation: for when he is tried, he shall receive the crown of life, which the Lord hath promised to them that love him.   *James 1:12*

Be thou faithful unto death, and I will give thee a crown of life.   *Revelation 2:10b*

And, behold, I come quickly; and my reward is with me, to give every man according as his work shall be.   *Revelation 22:12*

QUESTION 100
DID GOD WRITE THE BIBLE?

And the tables were the work of God, and the writing was the writing of God, graven upon the tables.   *Exodus 32:16*

And the LORD delivered unto me two tables of stone written with the finger of God; and on them was written according to all the words, which the LORD spake with you in the mount out of the midst of the fire in the day of the assembly.
Deuteronomy 9:10

As he spake by the mouth of his holy prophets, which have been since the world began: *Luke 1:70*

In the beginning was the Word, and the Word was with God, and the Word was God.
And the Word was made flesh, and dwelt among us, (and we beheld his glory, the glory as of the only begotten of the Father,) full of grace and truth.
John 1:1,14

(Which he had promised afore by his prophets in the holy scriptures.)
Concerning his Son Jesus Christ our Lord, which was made of the seed of David according to the flesh; *Romans 1:2,3*

All scripture is given by inspiration of God, and is profitable for doctrine, for reproof, for correction, for instruction in righteousness: *II Timothy 3:16*

For the prophecy came not in old time by the will of man: but holy men of God spake as they were moved by the Holy Ghost. *II Peter 1:21*

QUESTION 101 — WHY DO WE NEED TO STUDY THE BIBLE?

And these words, which I command thee this day, shall be in thine heart: *Deuteronomy 6:6*

But the word is very nigh unto thee, in thy mouth, and in thy heart, that thou mayest do it. *Deuteronomy 30:14*

This book of the law shall not depart out of thy mouth; but thou shalt meditate therein day and night, that thou mayest observe to do according to all that is written therein: for then thou shalt make thy way prosperous, and then thou shalt have good success. *Joshua 1:8*

Be ye mindful always of his covenant; the word which he commanded to a thousand generations; *I Chronicles 16:15*

Blessed is the man that walketh not in the counsel of the ungodly, nor standeth in the way of sinners, nor sitteth in the seat of the scornful.
But his delight is in the law of the LORD; and in his law doth he meditate day and night. *Psalms 1:1,2*

Wherewithal shall a young man cleanse his way? by taking heed thereto according to thy word.
Thy word have I hid in mine heart, that I might not sin against thee.
Unless thy law had been my delights, I should then have perished in mine affliction.
Thy word is a lamp unto my feet, and a light unto my path.
The entrance of thy words giveth light; it giveth understanding unto the simple. *Psalms 119:9,11,92,105,130*

My son, attend to my words; incline thine ear unto my sayings.

Let them not depart from thine eyes; keep them in the midst of thine heart.

For they are life unto those that find them, and health to all their flesh.   *Proverbs 4:20-22*

When thou goest, it shall lead thee; when thou sleepest, it shall keep thee; and when thou awakest, it shall talk with thee.

For the commandment is a lamp; and the law is light; and reproofs of instruction are the way of life: *Proverbs 6:22,23*

Study to shew thyself approved unto God, a workman that needeth not to be ashamed, rightly dividing the word of truth.
II Timothy 2:15

His Prosperity

QUESTION

102 DOES WEALTH COME FROM GOD OR SATAN?

But thou shalt remember the LORD thy God: for it is he that giveth thee power to get wealth, that he may establish his covenant which he sware unto thy fathers, as it is this day.

Deuteronomy 8:18

Praise ye the LORD. Blessed is the man that feareth the LORD, that delighteth greatly in his commandments.

His seed shall be mighty upon earth: the generation of the upright shall be blessed.

Wealth and riches shall be in his house: and his righteousness endureth for ever. *Psalms 112:1-3*

For the merchandise of it is better than the merchandise of silver, and the gain thereof than fine gold.

She is more precious than rubies: and all the things thou canst desire are not to be compared unto her.

Length of days is in her right hand; and in her left hand riches and honour. *Proverbs 3:14-16*

Riches and honour are with me; yea, durable riches and righteousness. *Proverbs 8:18*

By humility and the fear of the LORD are riches, and honour, and life. *Proverbs 22:4*

Every man also to whom God hath given riches and wealth, and hath given him power to eat thereof, and to take his portion, and to rejoice in his labour; this is the gift of God.

Ecclesiastes 5:19

But my God shall supply all your need according to his riches in glory by Christ Jesus.   *Philippians 4:19*

QUESTION 103 | WHAT DOES GOD WARN ABOUT WEALTH?

He that trusteth in his riches shall fall: but the righteous shall flourish as a branch.   *Proverbs 11:28*

Labour not to be rich: cease from thine own wisdom.
Wilt thou set thine eyes upon that which is not? for riches certainly make themselves wings; they fly away as an eagle toward heaven.   *Proverbs 23:4,5*

For the love of money is the root of all evil: which while some coveted after, they have erred from the faith, and pierced themselves through with many sorrows.
Charge them that are rich in this world, that they be not highminded, nor trust in uncertain riches, but in the living God, who giveth us richly all things to enjoy;
That they do good, that they be rich in good works, ready to distribute, willing to communicate;
Laying up in store for themselvers a good foundation against the time to come, that they may lay hold on eternal life.
I Timothy 6:10,17-19

QUESTION 104

WHO ARE MEN THAT GOD MADE FINANCIALLY WEALTHY?

And Abram was very rich in cattle, in silver, and in gold.
Genesis 13:2

And the LORD hath blessed my master greatly; and he is become great: and he hath given him flocks, and herds, and silver, and gold, and menservants, and maidservants, and camels, and asses.
Genesis 24:35

So king Solomon exceeded all the kings of the earth for riches and for wisdom.
I Kings 10:23

And God said to Solomon, Because this was in thine heart, and thou hast not asked riches, wealth, or honour, nor the life of thine enemies, neither yet hast asked long life; but hast asked wisdom and knowledge for thyself, that thou mayest judge my people, over whom I have made thee king:
Wisdom and knowledge is granted unto thee; and I will give thee riches, and wealth, and honour, such as none of the kings have had that have been before thee, neither shall there any after thee have the like.
II Chronicles 1:11-12

And king Solomon passed all the kings of the earth in riches and wisdom.
II Chronicles 9:22

There was a man in the land of Uz, whose name was Job; and that man was perfect and upright, and one that feared God, and eschewed evil.

and eschewed evil.

And there were born unto him seven sons and three daughters.

His substance also was seven thousand sheep, and and three thousand camels, and five hundred yoke of oxen, and five hundred she asses, and a very great household; so that this man was the greatest of all the men of the east.   *Job 1:1-3*

QUESTION 105
WHAT MUST I DO BEFORE GOD CAN PROMOTE ME?

Wisdom is the principal thing; therefore get wisdom: and with all thy getting get understanding.

Exalt her, and she shall promote thee: she shall bring thee to honour, when thou dost embrace her.

She shall give to thine head an ornament of grace: a crown of glory shall she deliver to thee.   *Proverbs 4:7-9*

He becometh poor that dealeth with a slack hand: but the hand of the diligent maketh rich.   *Proverbs 10:4*

The hand of the diligent shall bear rule: but the slothful shall be under tribute.

The slothful man roasteth not that which he took in hunting: but the substance of a diligent man is precious. *Proverbs 12:24,27*

The soul of the sluggard desireth, and hath nothing: but the soul of the diligent shall be made fat.   *Proverbs 13:4*

The thoughts of the diligent tend only to plenteousness; but of every one that is hasty only to want.   *Proverbs 21:5*

Seest thou a man diligent in his business? he shall stand before kings; he shall not stand before mean men.

Servants, be obedient to them that are your masters according to the flesh, with fear and trembling, in singleness of your heart, as unto Christ;

Not with eyeservice, as menpleasers; but as the servants of Christ, doing the will of God from the heart;

With good will doing service, as to the Lord, and not to men:

Knowing that whatsoever good thing any man doeth, the same shall he receive of the Lord, whether he be bond or free.

And, ye masters, do the same things unto them, forbearing threatening: knowing that your Master also is in heaven; neither is there respect of persons with him. *Ephesians 6:5-9*

QUESTION 106 — WHAT IS THE GOLDEN MASTER KEY IN CREATING A FLOW OF FINANCES INTO YOUR LIFE?

Happy is the man that findeth wisdom, and the man that getteth understanding.

For the merchandise of it is better than the merchandise of silver, and the gain thereof than fine gold.

She is more precious than rubies: and all the things thou canst desire are not to be compared unto her.

Length of days is in her right hand; and in her left hand riches and honour. *Proverbs 3:13-16*

There is that scattereth, and yet increaseth; and there is that withholdeth more than is meet, but it tendeth to poverty.

The liberal soul shall be made fat: and he that watereth shall be watered also himself.

He that withholdeth corn, the people shall curse him: but blessing shall be upon the head of him that selleth it.

Proverbs 11:24-26

Bring ye all the tithes into the storehouse, that there may be meat in mine house, and prove me now herewith, saith the LORD of hosts, if I will not open you the windows of heaven, and pour you out a blessing, that there shall not be room enough to receive it.

And I will rebuke the devourer for your sakes, and he shall not destroy the fruits of your ground; neither shall your vine cast her fruit before the time in the field, saith the LORD of hosts.

And all nations shall call you blessed: for ye shall be a delightsome land, saith the LORD of hosts. *Malachi 3:10-12*

Give, and it shall be given unto you; good measure, pressed down, and shaken together, and running over, shall men give into your bosom. For with the same measure that ye mete withal it shall be measured to you again. *Luke 6:38*

But this I say, He which soweth sparingly shall reap also sparingly; and he which soweth bountifully shall reap also bountifully. *II Corinthians 9:6*

QUESTION 107 — WILL GOD ALWAYS SUPPLY OUR NEEDS?

I have been young, and now am old; yet have I not seen the righteous forsaken, nor his seed begging bread. *Psalms 37:25*

Trust in the LORD, and do good; so shalt thou dwell in the land, and verily thou shalt be fed. *Psalms 37:3*

108 WHY DOES GOD ALLOW PROVERTY?

But it shall come to pass, if thou wilt not hearken unto the voice of the LORD thy God, to observe to do all his commandments and his statues which I command thee this day; that all these curses shall come upon thee, and overtake thee:

Cursed shalt thou be in the city, and cursed shalt thou be in field.

Cursed shall be thy basket and thy store.

Cursed shall be the fruit of thy body, and the fruit of thy land, the increase of thy kine, and the flocks of thy sheep.

Cursed shalt thou be when thou comest in, and cursed shalt thou be when thou goest out.   *Deuteronomy 28:15-19*

For by means of a whorish woman a man is brought to a piece of bread: *Proverbs 6:26a*

He becometh poor that dealeth with a slack hand: but the hand of the diligent maketh rich.   *Proverbs 10:4*

There is that scattereth, and yet increaseth; and there is that withholdeth more than is meet, but it tendeth to poverty.

The liberal soul shall be made fat: and he that watereth shall be watered also himself.

He that withholdeth corn, the people shall curse him: but blessing shall be upon the head of him that selleth it.

He that trusteth in his riches shall fall: but the righteous shall flourish as a branch.   *Proverbs 11:24-26,28*

The hand of the diligent shall bear rule: but the slothful shall be under tribute.   *Proverbs 12:24*

The soul of the sluggard desireth, and hath nothing: but the soul of the diligent shall be made fat.

Wealth gotten by vanity shall be diminished: but he that gathereth by labour shall increase.

Poverty and shame shall be to him that refuseth instruction: but he that regardeth reproof shall be honoured.

Proverbs 13:4,11,18

He that oppresseth the poor to increase his riches, and he that giveth to the rich, shall surely come to want. *Proverbs 22:16*

Through wisdom is an house builded; and by understanding it is established:

And by knowledge shall the chambers be filled with all precious and pleasant riches.

Yet a little sleep, a little slumber, a little folding of the hands to sleep:

So shall thy poverty come as one that travelleth; and thy want as an armed man. *Proverbs 24:3-4,33-34*

My people are destroyed for lack of knowledge: because thou hast rejected knowledge, I will also reject thee, that thou shalt be no priest to me: seeing thou hast forgotten the law of thy God, I will also forget thy children. *Hosea 4:6*

Ye ask, and receive not, because ye ask amiss, that ye may consume it upon your lusts. *James 4:3*

20
His Protection Of His Children

109
DID GOD MAKE ANY SPECIAL PROMISES OF PROTECTION?

The LORD is my light and my salvation; whom shall I fear? the LORD is the strength of my life; of whom shall I be afraid?

Though an host should encamp against me, my heart shall not fear: though war should rise against me, in this will I be confident. *Psalms 27:1,3*

He that dwelleth in the secret place of the most High shall abide under the shadow of the Almighty.

He shall cover thee with his feathers, and under his wings shalt thou trust: his truth shall be thy shield and buckler.

Thou shalt not be afraid for the terror by night; nor for the arrow that flieth by day;

Nor for the pestilence that walketh in darkness; nor for the destruction that wasteth at noonday.

A thousand shall fall at thy side, and ten thousand at thy right hand; but it shall not come nigh thee. *Psalms 91:1,4-7*

There shall no evil befall thee, neither shall any plague come nigh thy dwelling.

For he shall give his angels charge over thee, to keep thee in all thy ways. *Psalms 91:10,11*

all thy ways. *Psalms 91:10,11*

Be not afraid of sudden fear, neither of the desolation of the wicked, when it cometh.

For the LORD shall be thy confidence, and shall keep thy foot from being taken. *Proverbs 3:25,26*

In righteousness shalt thou be established: thou shalt be far from oppression; for thou shalt not fear: and from terror; for it shall not come near thee., *Isaiah 54:14*

QUESTION 110 DO ANGELS PLAY A PART IN MY PROTECTION?

There shall no evil befall thee, neither shall any plague come nigh thy dwelling.

For he shall give his angels charge over thee, to keep thee in all thy ways.

They shall bear thee up in their hands, lest thou dash thy foot against a stone. *Psalms 91:10-12*

And at that time shall Michael stand up, the great prince which standeth for the children of thy people: and there shall be a time of trouble, such as never was since there was a nation even to that same time: and at that time thy people shall be delivered, every one that shall be found written in the book. *Daniel 12:1*

And then shall he send his angels, and shall gather together his elect from the four winds, from the uttermost part of the earth to the uttermost part of heaven. *Mark 13:27*

Are they not all ministering spirits, sent forth to minister for them who shall be heirs of salvation? *Hebrews 1:14*

HIS PROTECTION OF HIS CHILDREN

QUESTION
111 WHAT ARE ANGELS?

And again, when he bringeth in the firstbegotten into the world, he saith, And let all the angels of God worship him.

And of the angels he saith, Who maketh his angels spirits, and his ministers a flame of fire.   *Hebrews 1:6,7*

The mystery of the seven stars which thou sawest in my right hand, and the seven golden candlesticks. The seven stars are the angels of the seven churches: and the seven candlesticks which thou sawest are the seven churches.   *Revelation 1:20*

QUESTION
112 ARE THERE DIFFERENT KINDS OF ANGELS?

So he drove out the man; and he placed at the east of the garden of Eden Cherubims, and a flaming sword which turned every way, to keep the way of the tree of life.   *Genesis 3:24*

Who maketh his angels spirits; his ministers a flaming fire:
Psalms 104:4

Above it stood the seraphims: each one had six wings; with twain he covered his face, and with twain he covered his feet, and with twain he did fly.   *Isaiah 6:2*

Yea, whiles I was speaking in prayer, even the man Gabriel, whom I had seen in the vision at the beginning, being caused to fly swiftly, touched me about the time of the evening oblation.
Daniel 9:21

But, lo, Michael, one of the chief princes, came to help me; and I remained there with the kings of Persia.   *Daniel 10:13b*

And at that time shall Michael stand up, the great prince which standeth for the children of thy people: *Daniel 12:1a*

And the angel answering said unto him, I am Gabriel, that stand in the presence of God; and am sent to speak unto thee, and to shew thee these glad tidings.

And in the sixth month the angel Gabriel was sent from God unto a city of Galilee, named Nazareth,   *Luke 1:19,26*

Yet Michael the archangel, when contending with the devil he disputed about the body of Moses, durst not bring against him a railing accusation, but said, The Lord rebuke thee.
                                                              Jude 1:9

And there was war in heaven: Michael and his angels fought against the dragon; and the dragon fought and his angels,
                                                    Revelation 12:7

QUESTION 113 IS IT TRUE THAT MY OBEDIENCE AND EVEN MY OFFERINGS TO GOD INFLUENCE HIS REACTION TO MY ENEMIES?

If ye walk in my statutes, and keep my commandments, and do them;

And ye shall chase your enemies, and they shall fall before you by the sword.

And five of you shall chase an hundred, and an hundred of you shall put ten thousand to flight: and your enemies shall fall before you by the sword.   *Leviticus 26:3,7,8*

HIS PROTECTION OF HIS CHILDREN

Bring ye all the tithes into the storehouse, that there may be meat in mine house, and prove me now herewith, saith the LORD of hosts, if I will not open you the windows of heaven, and pour you out a blessing, that there shall not be room enough to receive it.

And I will rebuke the devourer for your sakes, and he shall not destroy the fruits of your ground; neither shall your vine cast her fruit before the time in the field, saith the LORD of hosts.

And all nations shall call you blessed: for ye shall be a delightsome land, saith the LORD of hosts.   *Malachi 3:10-12*

His Purity

HAS GOD EVER TOLD A LIE?

God is not a man, that he should lie; neither the son of man, that he should repent; hath he said, and shall he not do it? or hath he spoken, and shall he not make it good?

Numbers 23:19

For men verily swear by the greater: and an oath for confirmation is to them an end of all strife.

Wherein God, willing more abundantly to shew unto the heirs of promise the immutability of his counsel, confirmed it by an oath:

That by two immutable things, in which it was impossible for God to lie, we might have a strong consolation, who have fled for refuge to lay hold upon the hope set before us:

Hebrews 6:16-18

WHAT DOES GOD HATE?

Neither shalt thou set thee up any image; which the LORD thy God hateth.   *Deuteronomy 16:22*

Thou lovest righteousness, and hatest wickedness: therefore God, thy God, hath anointed thee with the oil of gladness above thy fellows.   *Psalms 45:7*

These six things doth the LORD hate: yea, seven are an abomination unto him:

A proud look, a lying tongue, and hands that shed innocent blood,

An heart that deviseth wicked imaginations, feet that be swift in running to mischief,

A false witness that speaketh lies, and he that soweth discord among brethren.

My son, keep thy father's commandment, and forsake not the law of thy mother: *Proverbs 6:16-20*

Thou hast loved righteousness, and hated iniquity; therefore God, even thy God, hath anointed thee with the oil of gladness above thy fellows.   *Hebrews 1:9*

QUESTION 116 WHAT IS GOD'S REACTION TO SEXUAL SIN?

Thou shalt not commit adultery.   *Exodus 20:14*

Neither yield ye your members as instruments of unrighteousness unto sin: but yield yourselves unto God, as those that are alive from the dead, and your members as instruments of righteousness unto God.   *Romans 6:13*

What? know ye not that your body is the temple of the Holy Ghost which is in you, which ye have of God, and ye are not your own?

For ye are bought with a price: therefore glorify God in your body, and in your spirit, which are God's.

I Corinthians 6:19,20

But I keep under my body, and bring it into subjection: lest that by any means, when I have preached to others, I myself should be a castaway. *I Corinthians 9:27*

But fornication, and all uncleanness, or covetousness, let it not be once named among you, as becometh saints;
Ephesians 5:3

Abstain from all appearance of evil. *I Thessalonians 5:22*

22

His Purpose For Man On Earth

QUESTION
117
WHAT DID GOD CREATE FIRST?

In the beginning God created the heaven and the earth.

Genesis 1:1

QUESTION
118
WHAT IS THE PURPOSE OF GOD'S WORD?

He sent his word, and healed them, and delivered them from their destructions.　　　*Psalms 107:20*

Wherewithal shall a young man cleanse his way? by taking heed thereto according to thy word.　　　*Psalms 119:9*

And beginning at Moses and all the prophets, he expounded unto them in all the scriptures the things concerning himself.

Luke 24:27

Search the scriptures; for in them ye think ye have eternal life: and they are they which testify of me.　　　*John 5:39*

These things have I spoken unto you, that my joy might remain in you, and that your joy might be full.　　　*John 15:11*

And now come I to thee; and these things I speak in the world, that thy might have my joy fulfilled in themselves.

John 17:13

For he mightily convinced the Jews, and that publickly, showing by the scriptures that Jesus was Christ.   *Acts 18:28*

For whatsoever things were written aforetime were written for our learning, that we through patience and comfort of the scriptures might have hope.   *Romans 15:4*

And that from a child thou hast known the holy scriptures, which are able to make thee wise unto salvation through faith which is in Christ Jesus.

All scripture is given by inspiration of God, and is profitable for doctrine, for reproof, for correction, for instruction in righteousness:

That the man of God may be perfect, thoroughly furnished unto all good works.   *II Timothy 3:15-17*

For the word of God is quick, and powerful, and sharper than any twoedged sword, piercing even to the dividing asunder of soul and spirit, and of the joints and marrow, and is a discerner of the thoughts and intents of the heart.   *Hebrews 4:12*

QUESTION 119 HOW DO I KNOW I AM IMPORTANT TO GOD?

Doth not he see my ways, and count all my steps? *Job 31:4*

Behold, the eye of the LORD is upon them that fear him, upon them that hope in his mercy;   *Psalms 33:18*

Yet the Lord will command his lovingkindness in the daytime, and in the night his song shall be with me, and my prayer unto the God of my life.   *Psalms 42:8*

For he knoweth our frame; he remembereth that we are dust.   *Psalms 103:14*

For thou hast possessed my reins: thou hast covered me in my mother's womb.

I will praise thee; for I am fearfully and wonderfully made: marvelous are thy works; and that my soul knoweth right well.

My substance was not hid from thee, when I was made in secret, and curiously wrought in the lowest parts of the earth.

Thine eyes did see my substance, yet being unperfect; and in thy book all my members were written, which in continuance were fashioned, when as yet there was none of them.

How precious also are thy thoughts unto me, O God! how great is the sum of them!

If I should count them, they are more in number than the sand: when I awake, I am still with thee.   *Psalms 139:13-18*

Behold, I have graven thee upon the palms of my hands;
                                            Isaiah 49:16a

Before I formed thee in the belly I knew thee; and before thou camest forth out of the womb I sanctified thee, and I ordained thee a prophet unto the nations.   *Jeremiah 1:5*

Behold the fowls of the air: for they sow not, neither do they reap, nor gather into barns; yet your heavenly Father feedeth them. Are ye not much better than they?   *Matthew 6:26*

But the very hairs of your head are all numbered.
                                            Matthew 10-30

For God so loved the world, that he gave his only begotten Son, that whosoever believeth in him should not perish, but have everlasting life.   *John 3:16*

Nevertheless the foundation of God standeth sure, having this seal, The Lord knoweth them that are his.   *II Timothy 2:19*

Casting all your care upon him; for he careth for you.
I Peter 5:7

We love him, because he first loved us.   *I John 4:19*

23

His Pursuit
Of Man

120 | DOES GOD GIVE
GIFTS TO US?

But thou shalt remember the LORD thy God: for it is he that giveth thee power to get wealth, that he may establish his covenant which he sware unto the fathers, as it is this day.

Deuteronomy 8:18

Blessed be the Lord, who daily loadeth us with benefits, even the God our salvation. Selah.   *Psalms 68:19*

Bless, the LORD, O my soul, and forget not all his benefits:
Who forgiveth all thine iniquities; who healeth all thy diseases;
Who redeemeth thy life from destruction; who crowneth thee with lovingkindness and tender mercies;
Who satisfieth thy mouth with good things; so that thy youth is renewed like the eagle's.   *Psalms 103:2-5*

Who giveth food to all flesh: for his mercy endureth for ever.   *Psalms 136:25*

Bring ye all the tithes into the storehouse, that there may be meat in mine house, and prove me now herewith, saith the LORD of hosts, if I will not open you the windows of heaven, and pour you out a blessing, that there shall not be room enough to receive it.

And I will rebuke the devourer for your sakes, and he shall not destroy the fruits of your ground; neither shall your vine cast her fruit before the time in the field, saith the LORD of hosts.

And all nations shall call you blessed: for ye shall be a delightsome land, saith the LORD of hosts. *Malachi 3:10-12*

Ask, and it shall be given you; seek, and ye shall find; knock, and it shall be opened unto you:

For every one that asketh receiveth; and he that seeketh findeth; and to him that knocketh it shall be opened.

Or what man is there of you, whom if his son ask bread, will he give him a stone?

Or if he ask a fish, will he give him a serpent?

If ye then, being evil, know how to give good gifts unto your children, how much more shall your Father which is in heaven give good things to them that ask him?

Matthew 7:7-11

Give, and it shall be given unto you; good measure, pressed down, and shaken together, and running over, shall men give into your bosom. For with the same measure that ye mete withal it shall be measured to you again. *Luke 6:38*

Jesus answered and said unto her, If thou knewest the gift of God, and who it is that saith to thee, Give me to drink; thou wouldest have asked of him, and he would have given thee living water. *John 4:10*

Then Peter said unto them, Repent, and be baptized every one of you in the name of Jesus Christ for the remission of sins, and ye shall receive the gift of the Holy Ghost. *Acts 2:38*

For the wages of sin is death; but the gift of God is eternal life through Jesus Christ our Lord. *Romans 6:23*

Thanks be unto God for his unspeakable gift.

II Corinthians 9:15

For by grace are ye saved through faith; and that not of yourselves: it is the gift of God. *Ephesians 2:8*

But unto everyone of us is given grace according to the measure of the gift of Christ.

Wherefore he saith, When he ascended up on high, he led captivity captive, and gave gifts unto men. *Ephesians 4:7-8*

Every good gift and every perfect gift is from above, and cometh down from the Father of lights, with whom is no variableness, neither shadow of turning. *James 1:17*

QUESTION 121 IS THERE LIFE AFTER DEATH?

If a man die, shall he live again? all the days of my appointed time will I wait, till my change come. *Job 14:14*

Let not your heart be troubled: ye believe in God, believe also in me.

In my Father's house are many mansions: if it were not so, I would have told you. I go to prepare a place for you.

And if I go and prepare a place for you, I will come again, and receive you unto myself; that where I am, there ye may be also. *John 14:1-3*

If in this life only we have hope in Christ, we are of all men most miserable.

For as in Adam all die, even so in Christ shall all be made alive.

The last enemy that shall be destroyed is death.

And as we have borne the image of the earthy, we shall also bear the image of the heavenly.   *I Corinthians 15:19,22,26,49*

But I would not have you to be ignorant, brethren, concerning them which are asleep, that ye sorrow not, even as others which have no hope.

For if we believe that Jesus died and rose again, even so them also which sleep in Jesus will God bring with him.

For this we say unto you by the word of the Lord, that we which are alive and remain unto the coming of the Lord shall not prevent them which are asleep.

For the Lord himself shall descend from heaven with a shout, with the voice of the archangel, and with the trump of God: and in the dead in Christ shall rise first:

Then we which are alive and remain shall be caught up together with them in the clouds, to meet the Lord in the air: and so shall we ever be with the Lord.

Wherefore comfort one another with these words.
I Thessalonians 4:13-18

And as it is appointed unto men once to die, but after this the judgment: *Hebrews 9:27*

And God shall wipe away all tears from their eyes; and there shall be no more death, neither sorrow, nor crying, neither shall there be any more pain: for the former things are passed away.
Revelation 21:4

122 DOES GOD KNOW MY VERY THOUGHTS?

And GOD saw that the wickedness of man was great in the earth, and that every imagination of the thoughts of his heart was only evil continually.
Genesis 6:5

For I know their imagination which they go about, even now, before I have brought them into the land which I sware.
Deuteronomy 31:21b

For thou only knowest the hearts of the children of men:
II Chronicles 6:30b

I know that thou canst do every thing, and that no thought can be witholden from thee.
Job 42:2

Shall not God search this out? for he knoweth the secrets of the heart.
Psalms 44:21

The LORD knoweth the thoughts of man, that they are vanity.
Psalms 94:11

O LORD, thou hast searched me, and known me.

Thou knowest my downsitting and mine uprising, thou understandest my thought afar off.

Thou compassest my path and my lying down, and art acquainted with all my ways.

For there is not a word in my tongue, but, lo, O LORD, thou knowest it altogether.

Thou hast beset me behind and before, and laid thine hand upon me.

Such knowledge is too wonderful for me; it is high, I cannot attain unto it.

Whither shall I go from thy spirit? or whither shall I flee from thy presence?

If I ascend up into heaven, thou art there: if I make my bed in hell, behold, thou art there.

If I take the wings of the morning, and dwell in the uttermost parts of the sea;

Even there shall thy hand lead me, and thy right hand shall hold me.

If I say, Surely the darkness shall cover me; even the night shall be light about me.

Yea, the darkness hideth not from thee; but the night shineth as the day: the darkness and the light are both alike to thee.

For thou hast possessed my reins: thou hast covered me in my mother's womb.

I will praise thee; for I am fearfully and wonderfully made: marvelous are thy works; and that my soul knoweth right well.

My substance was not hid from thee, when I was made in secret, and curiously wrought in the lowest parts of the earth.

Thine eyes did see my substance, yet being unperfect; and in thy book all my members were written, which in continuance were fashioned, when as yet there was none of them.

How precious also are thy thoughts unto me, O God! how great is the sum of them!

If I should count them, they are more in number than the sand: when I awake, I am still with thee.

Search me, O God, and know my heart: try me, and know my thoughts:

And see if there be any wicked way in me, and lead me in the way everlasting.   *Psalms 139:1-18,23,24*

But he, knowing their thoughts, said unto them, Every kingdom divided against itself is brought to desolation; and a house divided against a house falleth.   *Luke 11:17*

And again, The Lord knoweth the thoughts of the wise, that they are vain.   *I Corinthians 3:20*

QUESTION 123

DOES GOD WANT ME TO ENJOY LIFE?

And it shall come to pass, if thou shalt hearken diligently unto the voice of the LORD thy God, to observe and to do all his commandments which I command thee this day, that the LORD thy God will set thee on high above all nations of the earth:

And all these blessings shall come on thee, and overtake thee, if thou shalt hearken unto the voice of the LORD thy God.

Blessed shalt thou be in the city, and blessed shalt thou be in the field.

Blessed shall be the fruit of thy body, and the fruit of thy ground, and the fruit of thy cattle, the increase of thy kine, and the flocks of thy sheep.

Blessed shall be thy basket and thy store.

Blessed shalt thou be when thou comest in, and blessed shalt thou be when thou goest out.

The LORD shall cause thine enemies that rise up against thee to be smitten before thy face: they shall come out against thee one way, and flee before thee seven ways.

The LORD shall command the blessing upon thee in thy storehouses, and in all that thou settest thine hand unto; and he shall bless thee in the land which the LORD thy God giveth thee.

The LORD shall establish thee an holy people unto himself, as he hath sworn unto thee, if thou shalt keep the commandments of the LORD thy God, and walk in his ways.

And all people of the earth shall see that thou art called by the name of the LORD; and they shall be afraid of thee.

The LORD shall make thee plenteous in goods, in the fruit of thy body, and in the fruit of thy cattle, and in the fruit of thy ground, in the land which the LORD sware unto thy fathers to give thee.

The LORD shall open up unto thee his good treasure, the heaven to give the rain unto thy land in his season, and to bless all the work of thine hand: and thou shalt lend unto many nations, and thou shalt not borrow.

And the LORD shall make thee the head, and not the tail; and thou shalt be above only, and thou shalt not be beneath; if that thou hearken unto the commandments of the LORD thy God, which I command thee this day, to observe and to do them:

And thou shalt not go aside from any of the words which I command thee this day, to the right hand, or to the left, to go after other gods to serve them. *Deuteronomy 28:1-14*

Thou wilt shew me the path of life: in thy presence is fullness of joy; at thy right hand there are pleasures for evermore.
Psalms 16:11

For the LORD God is a sun and shield: the LORD will give grace and glory: no good thing will he withhold from them that walk uprightly. *Psalms 84:11*

Behold that which I have seen: it is good and comely for one to eat and to drink, and to enjoy the good of all his labour that he taketh under the sun all the days of his life, which God giveth him: for it is his portion. *Ecclesiastes 5:18*

Therefore with joy shall ye draw water out of the wells of salvation. *Isaiah 12:3*

They shall not build, and another inhabit; they shall not plant, and another eat: for as the days of a tree are the days of my people, and mine elect shall long enjoy the work of their hands. *Isaiah 65:22*

Ask, and it shall be given you; seek, and ye shall find; knock, and it shall be opened unto you:

For every one that asketh receiveth; and he that seeketh findeth; and to him that knocketh it shall be opened.

Or what man is there of you, whom if his son ask bread, will he give him a stone?

Or if he ask a fish, will he give him a serpent?

I ye then, being evil, know how to give good gifts unto your children, how much more shall your Father which is in heaven give good things to them that ask him?   *Matthew 7:7-11*

The thief cometh not, but for to steal, and to kill, and to destroy: I am come that they might have life, and that they might have it more abundantly.   *John 10:10*

These things have I spoken unto you, that my joy might remain in you, and that your joy might be full.   *John 15:11*

Hitherto have ye asked nothing in my name: ask, and ye shall receive, that your joy may be full.   *John 16:24*

Charge them that are rich in this world, that they be not highminded, nor trust in uncertain riches, but in the living God, who giveth us richly all things to enjoy;   *I Timothy 6:17*

QUESTION 124 IS IT POSSIBLE TO HAVE A PERSONAL RELATIONSHIP WITH GOD?

And I will give thee the treasures of darkness, and hidden riches of secret places, that thou mayest know that I, the LORD, which call thee by thy name, am the God of Israel.   *Isaiah 45:3*

153

Fear not: for I have redeemed thee, I have called thee by thy name; thou art mine.

Even every one that is called by my name: for I have created him for my glory, I have formed him; yea, I have made him.

This people have I formed for myself; they shall shew forth my praise. *Isaiah 43:1b,7,21*

And I will give them an heart to know me, that I am the LORD: and they shall be my people, and I will be their God: for they shall return unto me with their whole heart.

Jeremiah 24:7

For the Son of man is come to seek and to save that which was lost. *Luke 19;10*

But as many as received him, to them gave he power to become the sons of God, even to them that believe on his name: *John 1:12*

And because ye are sons, God hath sent forth Spirit of his Son into your hearts, crying, Abba, Father.

Wherefore thou art no more a servant, but a son; and if a son, then an heir of God through Christ. *Galatians 4:6,7*

DOES GOD REALLY REQUIRE THAT A PERSON BELIEVE IN JESUS CHRIST?

For God so loved the world, that he gave his only begotten Son, that whosoever believeth in him should not perish, but have everlasting life.

He that believeth on him is not condemned: but he that believeth not is condemned already, because he hath not believed in the name of the only begotten Son of God.

in the name of the only begotten Son of God.

He that believeth on the Son hath everlasting life: and he that believeth not the Son shall not see life; but the wrath of God abideth on him.   *John 3:16,18,36*

Verily, verily, I say unto you, He that entereth not by the door into the sheepfold, but climbeth up some other way, the same is a thief and a robber.

Then said Jesus unto them again, Verily, verily, I say unto you, I am the door of the sheep.

All that ever came before me are thieves and robbers: but the sheep did not hear them.

I am the door: by me if any man enter in, he shall be saved, and shall go in and out, and find pasture.

The thief cometh not, but for to steal, and to kill, and to destroy: I am come that they might have life, and that they might have it more abundantly.

I am the good shepherd: the good shepherd giveth his life for the sheep.   *John 10:1,7-11*

For the wages of sin is death; but the gift of God is eternal life through Jesus Christ our Lord.   *Romans 6;23*

He that believeth on the Son of God hath the witness in himself: he that believeth not God hath made him a liar; because he believeth not the record that God gave of his Son.

He that hath the Son hath life; and he that hath not the Son of God hath not life.   *I John 5:10,12*

QUESTION 126 WILL GOD ACCEPT ME IF I SIMPLY LIVE A GOOD AND MORAL LIFE?

Verily every man at his best state is altogether vanity.

But we are all as an unclean thing, and all our righteousnesses are as filthy rags; and we all do fade as a leaf; and our iniquities, like the wind, have taken us away. *Isaiah 64:6*

And when he was gone forth into the way, there came one running, and kneeled to him, and asked him, Good Master, what shall I do that I may inherit eternal life?

And Jesus said unto him, Why callest thou me good? there is none good but one, that is, God.

Thou knowest the commandments, Do not commit adultery, Do not kill, Do not steal, Do not bear false witness, Defraud not, Honour thy father and mother.

And he answered and said unto him, Master, all these have I observed from my youth.

Then Jesus beholding him loved him, and said unto him, One thing thou lackest: go thy way, sell whatsoever thou hast, and give to the poor, and thou shalt have treasure in heaven: and come, take up the cross, and follow me.

And he was sad at that saying, and went away grieved: for he had great possessions. *Mark 10:17-22*

For all have sinned, and come short of the glory of God; *Romans 3:23*

QUESTION 127 HOW DOES A PERSON BECOME A CHRISTIAN?

But as many as received him, to them gave he power to become the sons of God, even to them that believe on his name: John 1:12

For God so loved the world, that he sent his only begotten Son, that whosoever believeth in him should not perish, but have everlasting life.

And it shall come to pass, that whosoever shall call on the name of the Lord shall be saved.   *Acts 2:21*

But we believe that through the grace of the Lord Jesus Christ we shall be saved, even as they.   *Acts 15:11*

And brought them out, and said, Sirs, what must I do to be saved?

And they said, Believe on the Lord Jesus Christ, and thou shalt be saved, and thy house.   *Acts 16:30,31*

That if thou shalt confess with my mouth the Lord Jesus, and shalt believe in thine heart that God hath raised him from the dead, thou shalt be saved.

For with the heart man believeth unto righteousness; and with the mouth confession is made unto salvation.

For the scripture saith, Whosoever believeth on him shall not be ashamed.

For there is no difference between the Jew and the Greek: for the same Lord over all is rich unto all that call upon him.

For whosoever shall call upon the name of the Lord shall be saved.   *Romans 10:9-13*

For by grace are ye saved through faith; and that not of yourselves: it is the gift of God: *Ephesians 2:8*

But without faith it is impossible to please him: for he that cometh to God must believe that he is, and that he is a rewarder of them that diligently seek him.   *Hebrews 11:6*

These things have I written unto you that believe on the name of the Son of God; that ye may know that ye have eternal life, and that ye may believe on the name of the Son of God.

I John 5:13

ABOUT MIKE MURDOCK

► Has embraced his assignment to pursue...possess...and publish the Wisdom of God to heal the broken in his generation.

► Preached his first public sermon at the age of 8.

► Preached his first evangelistic crusade at the age of 15.

► Began full-time evangelism at the age of 19, in which he has continued for 28 years.

► Has traveled and spoken to more than 11,000 audiences in 36 countries, including East Africa, the Orient, and Europe.

► Receives more than 1,500 invitation each year to speak in churches, colleges, and business corporations.

► Noted author of 57 books, including the best sellers, "Wisdom for Winning", "Dream-Seeds", and "The Double Diamond Principle".

► Created the popular "Wisdom Topical Bible" series for Businessmen, Mothers, Fathers, Teenagers, and the One-Minute Pocket Bible.

► Has composed more than 1,200 songs such as "I Am Blessed", "You Can Make It", and "Jesus Just The Mention of Your Name", recorded by many gospel artists.

► He has released over 20 music albums as well, and the music video, "Going Back To The Word".

► Is a dynamic teacher having produced to date 21 Wisdom Teaching Tape series and 9 School of Wisdom videos.

► He has appeared often on TBN, CBN, and other television network programs.

► Is a Founding Trustee on the Board of Charismatic Bible Ministries.

► Is the Founder of the Wisdom Training Center, for the training of those entering the ministry.

► Has had more than 3,400 accept the call into full-time ministry under his ministry.

► Has a goal of establishing Wisdom Rooms in one million Christian homes.

► Has a weekly television program called "Wisdom for Crisis Times".

MY DECISION PAGE

May I Invite You To Make Jesus The Lord of Your Life?

The Bible says,"that if thou shalt confess with thy mouth the Lord Jesus Christ, and shalt believe in thine heart that God hath raised him from the dead, thou shalt be saved. For with the heart man believeth unto righteousness; and with the mouth confession is made unto salvation." (Romans 10:9,10)

To receive Jesus Christ as Lord and Saviour of your life, please pray this prayer from your heart today!

Dear Jesus,
    I believe that You died for me and that You arose again on the third day. I confess to You that I am a sinner and that I need Your love and forgiveness. Come into my life, forgive my sins, and give me eternal life. I confess You now as my Saviour! I walk in your peace and joy from this day forward.

Signed _____

Date _____

☐ Yes, Mike, I have accepted Christ as my personal Saviour and would like to receive my personal gift copy of your book *31 Keys To A New Beginning.* (B 48) #DC10

Name _____
Address _____
City _____ State _____ Zip_____
Phone (   )_____ Birthdate_____
Occupation_____

YOUR LETTER IS VERY IMPORTANT TO ME

Y ou are a special person to me, and I believe you are special to God. I want to help you in every way I can. Let me hear from you when you are facing spiritual needs or experiencing a conflict in your life, or if you just want to know that someone really cares. Write me. I will pray for your needs. And I will write you back something that I know will help you receive the miracle you need.

Mike, here are my special needs at this time:
-Please Print-

_____

_____

_____

_____

_____

_____

_____

_____

_____

_____

_____

_____

_____

Mail To:
MIKE MURDOCK
The Wisdom Center • P.O. Box 99 • Dallas, Texas 75221

WILL YOU BECOME A WISDOM KEY PARTNER?

1. TELEVISION - The Way Of The Winner, a nationally-syndicated weekly TV program features Mike Murdock's teaching and music.

2. WTC - Wisdom Training Center where Dr. Murdock trains those preparing for full-time ministry in a special 70 Hour Training Program.

3. MISSIONS - Recent overseas outreaches include crusades to East Africa, Brazil and Poland; 1,000 Young Minister's Handbooks sent to India to train nationals for ministry to their people..

4. MUSIC - Millions of people have been blessed by the anointed song-writing and singing talents of Mike Murdock, who has recorded over 20 highly-acclaimed albums.

5. LITERATURE - Best-selling books, teaching tapes and magazines proclaim the Wisdom of God.

6. CRUSADES - Multitudes are ministered to in crusades and seminars throughout America as Mike Murdock declares life-giving principles from God's Word.

7. SCHOOLS OF WISDOM - Each year Mike Murdock hosts Schools of Wisdom for those who want personalized and advanced training for achieving their dreams and goals.

I want to personally invite you to be a part of this ministry!

WISDOM KEY
PARTNERSHIP PLAN

Dear Partner,

God has brought us together! I love representing you as I spread His Wisdom in the world. Will you become my Faith-Partner? Your Seed is powerful. When you sow, three benefits are guaranteed:
PROTECTION (Mal. 3:10-11), FAVOR (Luke 6:38), FINANCIAL PROSPERITY (Deut. 8:18). *Please note the four levels as a monthly Wisdom Key Faith Partner. Complete the response sheet and rush it to me immediately. Then focus your expectations for the 100-fold return (Mark 10:30)!*

Your Faith Partner,

Mike Murdock

Yes, Mike, I want to be a Wisdom Key Partner with you. Please rush The Wisdom Key Partnership Pak to me today!

❑ **FOUNDATION PARTNER...**Yes, Mike, I want to be a Wisdom Key Foundation Partner. Enclosed is my first monthly Seed-Faith Promise of $15.

❑ **SEED-A-DAY...**Yes, Mike, I want to be a Wisdom Key Partner as a Seed-a-Day member. Enclosed is my first monthly Seed-Faith Promise of $30.

❑ **COVENANT OF BLESSING...**Yes, Mike, I want to be a Wisdom Key Partner as a Covenant of Blessing member. Enclosed is my first Seed-Faith Promise of $58.

❑ **THE SEVENTY...**Yes, Mike, I want to be a Wisdom Key Partner as a member of The Seventy. Enclosed is my first monthly Seed-Faith Promise of $100.

TOTAL ENCLOSED $ [   ] #DC10

Name _____

Address _____

City _____State _____Zip_____

Phone ( ) _____Birthday _____

Mail To:

MIKE MURDOCK

The Wisdom Center • P.O. Box 99 • Dallas, Texas 75221

163

WISDOM KEY PARTNERSHIP PAK

When you become a Wisdom Key Monthly Faith Partner or a part of The Seventy, you will receive our Partnership Pak which includes:

1. *Special Music Cassette*
2. *101 Wisdom Keys Book*
3. *Partnership Coupon Book*

Yes Mike! I Want To Be Your Partner!

❏ Enclosed is my best Seed-Faith Gift of $_____.

❏ I want to be a Wisdom Key Partner! Enclosed is my first Seed-Faith gift of $_____ for the first month.

❏ Please rush my special Partnership Pak. (#PP02)

Name _____

Address _____

City _____State _____Zip _____

Phone (   )_____

#DC10

Mail To:
MIKE MURDOCK
The Wisdom Center • P.O. Box 99 • Dallas, Texas 75221

4 POWER-PACKED TAPE SERIES BY MIKE MURDOCK

HOW TO WALK THROUGH FIRE

The 4 basic causes of conflict and how to react in a personal crisis, which are extremely helpful for those who are walking through the fires of marriage difficulty, divorce, depression, and financial adversity. (TS5) Six Tape Series

$30

THE ASSIGNMENT

Do you wonder why you are here? What are you to do? These tapes will unlock the hidden treasures inside you to fulfill the *Assignment* God has called you to. 160 Wisdom Keys that can reveal the purpose of God. (TS22) Six Tape Series

$30

WOMEN THAT MEN CANNOT FORGET

Discover the success secrets of two of the most remarkable women in history...and how their secrets can help you achieve your dreams and goals! Both men and women will enjoy these wisdom secrets from the lives of Ruth and Esther. (TS31)Six Tape Series

$30

THE GRASSHOPPER COMPLEX

A must for those who need more self-confidence! It reveals the secrets of overcoming every giant you face in achieving your personal dreams and goals. (TS3)Six Tape Series

$30

Order All Four Series & Pay Only $100

6 Wisdom Books

WISDOM FOR CRISIS TIMES

Discover the Wisdom Keys to dealing with tragedies, stress and times of crisis. Secrets that will unlock the questions in the  right way to react in life situations. (Paperback)

(BK08) 118 Pages.....$7

THE DOUBLE DIAMOND PRINCIPLE

58 Master Secrets For Total Success, in the life of Jesus that will help you achieve your dreams and goals. (Paperback)

(BK71) 118 Pages.....$7

SEEDS OF WISDOM

One-Year Daily Devotional. A 374 page devotional with topics on dreams and goals, relationships, miracles, prosperity and more! (Paperback)

(BK02) 374 Pages.....$10

WISDOM FOR WINNING

The best-selling handbook for achieving success. If you desire to be successful and happy, this is the book for you! (Paperback)

(BK23) 280 Pages.....$9

ONE-YEAR TOPICAL BIBLE

A One-Minute reference Bible. 365 topics; spiritual, topical and easy to read. A collection of Scriptures relating to specific topics that challenge and concern you. (Paperback)

(BK03) 374 Pages.....$10

DREAM SEEDS

What do you dream of doing with you life? What would you attempt to do if you knew it was impossible to fail? This 118-page book helps you answer these questions and much more! (Paperback)

(BK20) 118 Pages.....$7

ORDER FORM

Item No.	Name of Item	Quantity	Price Per Item	Total
#TS22	The Assignment Tapes		30.00	$
#TS5	How To Walk Through Fire Tapes		30.00	$
#TS3	The Grasshopper Complex Tapes		30.00	$
#TS3	Women Men Cannot Forget Tapes		30.00	$
	All 4 Tape Series For $100.00			$
#BK20	Dream Seeds Book		7.00	$
#BK23	Wisdom For Winning Book		9.00	$
#BK20	Seeds of Wisdom Book (374 Pgs)		10.00	$
#BK71	Double Diamond Principle Book		7.00	$
#BK08	Wisdom For Crisis Times Book		7.00	$
#BK03	One Minute Topical Bible (374 Pgs)		10.00	$
SORRY NO C.O.D's		Add 10% For Shipping		$
		(Canada add 20%)		$
		Enclosed is my Seed-Faith Gift for Your Ministry.		$
#DC10		Total Amount Enclosed		$

Please Print

Name

Address

City

State _____ Zip

Phone(hm) _____ (wk)

☐ Check ☐ Money Order ☐ Cash

☐ Visa ☐ MasterCard ☐ AMEX

Signature_____

Card#

Expiration Date _____

☐ Send Free Catalog & Free Subscription To Newsletter *Wisdom Talk*

Mail To:

MIKE MURDOCK

The Wisdom Center • P.O. Box 99 • Dallas, Texas 75221